Escaping the Iron Curtain: Finding My Destiny

Ladis Visner
with Pat Visner

Published by
Innovo Publishing, LLC
www.innovopublishing.com
1-888-546-2111

Providing Full-Service Publishing Services for
Christian Authors, Artists & Organizations: Hardbacks, Paperbacks,
eBooks, Audiobooks, Music & Film

ESCAPING THE IRON CURTAIN: FINDING MY DESTINY

Library of Congress Control Number: 2016939319
ISBN: 978-1-61314-281-3

Cover Design & Interior Layout: Innovo Publishing, LLC

Printed in the United States of America
U.S. Printing History
First Edition: July 2016

ENDORSEMENTS

"Beautiful, encouraging story of one man taking a chance. He left all he had behind to make his dream come true . . ."
—Lucie H., Czech Republic

"The desire for freedom is powerful. *Escaping the Iron Curtain: Finding My Destiny* expresses this perfectly through the life story of one man who dared to escape Communism. Schools should have this book as suggested reading. Shall we, in America, never forget the oppression in the world nor take for granted our country. Thank you, Mr. Visner, for the reminder."
—Rhonda S., Ohio

"*Escaping the Iron Curtain: Finding My Destiny* relates how Communism and oppression degrade people and ruin lives and countries. The Communist takeover of Czechoslovakia happened in the late 1940s, and Communism continues in this world today. The story of the escape is one of courage and determination and is mesmerizing. Mr. Visner has come a long way since arriving in America, and I am proud to know this man."
—Barbara K., Colorado

PREFACE

When I came to America, people I met asked me about my accent—"Where are you from?"—more from curiosity than a personal interest in me. I usually gave them a flip answer like, "China" while squinting my eyes, or "the South Bronx." I kept my life story to myself; it was too personal to share with just anyone. Most people had no idea about my life under Communism. The only ones who fully understood were other immigrants who had similar stories. But I knew if I spent most of my time with them, I would never grow or learn.

When I met Pat, she had never heard of Czechoslovakia. I talked about it and showed her pictures, but it was difficult for her to understand. Gradually, in conversations with trusted friends, I started talking about it more. They were fascinated, and Pat often mentioned she wished she'd had a recorder. We decided to write my biography, so she gathered stories and information. We wanted my family in Czechoslovakia and future generations to know what I went through and what life was like before the fall of Communism in 1989.

My family and friends back home assume we will visit every year because we have for so many years. But they don't fully know what I went through to get to this point. We want them to understand while they still can.

Already we have lost a brother-in-law, and my brother has dementia. It is too bad he won't be able to appreciate this book; he was a major influence in my dream of living in America.

Pat wrote from the standpoint of a person who knew nothing about Czechoslovakia. She attempted to describe everyday life while capturing my adventures and emotions.

My story is just one of many about people who decided to take the dangerous path of attempting to escape from their countries behind the Iron Curtain. This book is to honor all those who never gave up in their fight for freedom.

My prayer is that mankind will seek to defeat Communism and its oppression wherever it exists and that those who endured or died will never be forgotten.

—Ladis Visner

DEDICATION

This is the true story of my life, as accurately as I remember, or as I was told. I dedicate this book to my family and friends in America and Europe and to future generations around the world.

ACKNOWLEDGMENTS

Sincere thanks to my wife, Pat, for coming up with the idea for a book of my life. Her tenacity, persistence, love, and perseverance made this happen.

Thanks to family and friends who encouraged us.

And special thanks to God for protecting and guiding me on my unique life journey.

Growing Up

Chapter 1

Flying through the air, giggling with delight at three years old, I was being tossed about by a burly black corporal in General Patton's Third Army as my mother looked on. It was the end of April 1945, and the soldiers were stationed in Hluboka, in a region called Bohemia—after liberating the western part of Czechoslovakia in World War II.

They stayed in houses on the main street for three to four weeks until the front moved to Pilsen. Patton wanted to continue on to Prague to liberate the capital from the Germans, but a demarcation line—just east of Pilsen that had been established by the Russian and British and American generals—prevented him from doing so.

The soldiers joked with the local kids and passed out chewing gum and chocolate. My eleven-year-old brother washed dishes for them in an open air field kitchen, while my mother did laundry for them. She was rewarded with a fifty-pound sack of sugar—a rare commodity—which she shared with the neighbors.

Their machine guns were lined up in our hallway, and my brother even knew some of the soldiers' names. It was an exciting time for us kids. But as exciting as this flight was, none was more life changing than my escape from Communist Czechoslovakia.

I was raised in Hluboka, a small town twenty kilometers from the German border. There was little work available in my country then. Because of my dad's German ancestry, he was hired to work for a machinery plant in Regensburg Germany for the war effort. He lived there and came home about twice a month, bringing with him food supplies and clothing for us.

My mom worked in a textile factory, about three kilometers away, walking there and back year round in all kinds of weather, for many years.

In 1946, after World War II, we moved to Nyrsko in a border region called Sudetenland. It was a disputed area between Germany and Czechoslovakia, and the Czech government had expelled the German residents for collaborating and spying. They had twenty-four hours to leave and could take only three kilograms—about six pounds—of possessions with them. Basically only what they could carry in their hands. They left hundreds of beautiful villas vacant and fully furnished, which were then sold to military and government people who had connections.

On the other side of town, my dad bought our little house, which had two bedrooms, a kitchen with a cold water faucet, and a dry toilet in a closet. It had been built to house two families, but because we were four children, our family was allowed to live there alone. My parents slept in one bedroom and we four kids slept in the smaller bedroom. My brother and I shared a bed, and my two sisters shared another.

Dad got a job in a manufacturing plant named Okula that made eyeglasses and equipment to grind lenses. He worked with red dye, which was used for polishing the lenses, and he would come home covered in it.

Our kitchen had a wood-burning stove that was used for heat and for cooking. In the winter, we spent a lot of our time in the kitchen, and Mom always had something tasty to eat. She heated water on the stove to partially fill our bathtub for our twice-weekly baths. It would have taken too much water for separate baths, so we shared the water. The tin tub was portable, and we stood it up in the hallway next to a huge sauerkraut barrel when we weren't using it. In the summer we put it outside in our garden for the sun to warm up the water. Water was also heated to use in the washing machine. It would take Mother all day to do laundry, putting it through a wringer by hand and hanging it on a clothesline in our yard.

We did not have a refrigerator. Food was kept cool in a "cold room" in the middle of the house. Beer, milk, fruit, vegetables, and apples were there, including all the foods she had put up in jars. The walls were forty centimeters thick, and the tile floor throughout the house was always cold.

Dishes were washed in a sink that was in a drawer, which was rolled out of the cupboard. She poured warm water in, and sometimes soap, washed them, and then rinsed them in a bowl of cold water. When she finished, we tossed the water on our garden and rolled the sink back out of sight.

Before Okula was even built, Nyrsko had three plants that manufactured bricks. The man-made ponds that I had skated on in winter were known for their good clay. It was really sticky and was perfect for brick making. My friends and I used to make balls of this stuff, put a stick in it, and fling it at each other. They left a real mess on our clothes.

These brick-making plants had kilns—to bake the bricks—and tall chimneys. They had long-ago ceased operations, and the buildings stood vacant, just right for mischievous teenagers. One day, I dared to climb the chimney on the inside, while my friends just looked on.

It was about six stories tall and covered in soot. Part way up I took off my jacket and threw it down. I was afraid it would get caught on a loose brick or the ladder, but it didn't. The higher I climbed the looser the rungs became, and some were even missing. I finally made it to the top of the chimney. I was petrified but feeling macho since no one else had done that, and I let out a yell. It would have been easier to float down in a parachute, but I had to gingerly climb back down the same way, being very careful not to lose my footing. I was covered with soot but glad to be safely back on the ground.

Chapter 2

In 1946, national elections were held. Czechoslovakia was tired from war and looking for change. Communists promised that classes of people would be merged and everything would be shared, so there would be no "haves" and "have nots." They accused the ruling Democratic party and its leaders of conspiracy, and their international background and wartime connections with the West were regarded as high treason. The Communist party won the elections and made Klement Gottwald the head of the country.

A large number of popular socialists were arrested, as ordered by the Kremlin, and radicalized Communist tactics were established. Their grip on my country tightened and Czechoslovakia became a satellite of the Soviet Union.

Businesses were socialized and all private property was confiscated and under the power of the state. The once prosperous country slid into apathy. Buildings went into disrepair, and progress stopped. Business was done with greed, bribery, cheating, and murder. At the same time, capitalism was denounced as bad.

Successful auto businesses, like Skoda, Tatra, and Avia and a shoe manufacturer, Bata, and countless others could no longer make world-market-oriented decisions for their companies. Many fled the country to the West or South America to start over again.

By the time I was seven years old, the borders were closed. High officials and the elite could still travel, but common people were not allowed to leave. I was locked in my country. One way to escape the reality of Communism was by reading contraband adventure booklets called *Rodokaps*, about the American West, with beautiful women and cowboys. They took me to another world that I dreamed of visiting one day. They had been freely published until 1948 when the Communists outlawed such publications as an American invention, though they were written by a Czech author who had traveled to America.

My parents didn't know my brother got them for me, and I shared them with my trusted circle of friends. I secretly read them in the woods or in our attic by flashlight. Getting caught with them meant confiscation and a fine. An underground press continued to publish them until they were forced to shut down in 1950. Publishers were arrested, but copies of *Rodokaps* were still circulating underground.

The public address system in every town advised people to bring them and all their other antisocialist literature to the authorities, but we were learning not to trust them and no one I knew turned them in.

By then, some of the magazines were so used they were yellow and illegible. I read as much as I could, and the parts that I couldn't decipher I imagined my own story line. I remember thinking how great it would be to live in a place like those in the stories.

The heroes in the American West always beat the bad guys, and they were free to own big ranches with lots of land and animals. No one else controlled their lives and they always got the beautiful girl. In my heart, I knew a place like that must exist.

We used to trade *Rodokaps* for weapons too. When George Patton's Third Army was advancing into Bohemia, the escaping German soldiers discarded their weapons, pistols, rifles, and machine guns as they retreated. Once in a while we discovered them hidden in piles of firewood or in the mud of the riverbeds.

We weren't used to owning weapons, so finding or trading for them was exciting and scary. We would clean them up and secretly show them off to friends.

When I was thirteen, I went on a field trip with my classmates to Russia. My Russian language teacher was from there and organized it all. She wanted to show us a new tourist center, which had just opened and was designed to show how "advanced" Communism was and their great achievements. It took us a day and a half by train to get there.

We first were shown a grocery store that was supposed to operate on the honor system—something we had never heard of. Shoppers were expected to take what they wanted and leave the appropriate amount of money for it.

There were perfect displays of the same horrible food as in Czechoslovakia—lots of canned meat and fish, no fresh vegetables, a few prunes and apples. Perfect displays, but no shoppers.

Later on I heard the store had been stripped of everything, including the cash registers, which had no money in them. What a joke that idea was!

Next, we were shown a farm so immaculate and perfect, it did not look real. Every stalk of grain in the wheat field looked artificial. The barn was new and sterile. I think even the cows must have been warned to not make a mess or smell! The whole scene was so staged.

It obviously was propaganda, and I wanted to see the true life— how people really lived there. We were taken to a river to bathe and have fun. There was a village across from the river.

So, when the teacher wasn't looking, my friend and I decided to go see for ourselves what it was like. We waded across the very cold water, carrying our clothes, and we walked around the gray village. We saw thatched-roof homes, broken fences, and animals coming and going in houses: goats, pigs, chickens.

There were no cars, just wooden carts like from the last century. Some homes had only a dirt floor, no tile or wood. The townspeople gawked at us, obvious strangers, as if they expected us to rob them. We were almost immediately reported to the authorities. About an hour later, our teacher caught up with us and reprimanded us. We had just wanted to see the real Russia, not the fake perfect society they had staged.

When we got back home, our parents were contacted and the teacher threatened to have us thrown out of school, but thank God, we weren't. I told my friends what the truth was, though I had no pictures to verify it. I was beginning to realize that Communism was all lies and deceit.

I had another run-in with this same teacher one day while playing ice hockey. She was a fan of the game and was standing very close to the goal. I had the puck and precisely aimed it right at her, hitting her in her big, fat Russian coat. She accused me of doing it deliberately, but I said she had been too close to the goal. Guess she just didn't like me. It was mutual.

When I was growing up there were two Catholic churches at opposite ends of town that were never locked. A friend and I used to sneak into one and climb through the rafters up the bell tower. Kavka birds (ravens) built their nests there, and I would steal their eggs. Then we would make a campfire and boil them for a nice little snack.

Once when I got caught, part of my punishment was doing yard work on the church grounds. I must have done a good job because later I was asked to be an altar boy, which was a great honor to me.

I was twelve years old, and one of my duties was to assist the priest in administering the communion. Another boy and I used to sample the wafers and the red wine behind the altar. I was hoping God couldn't see me in the shadows there.

Under Communism, the church was allowed to exist as long as it was no threat to the government. Also the leaders wanted to show the "friendly face of Communism."

By then, there was widespread apathy toward religion; most people were atheists. Services were attended by only a few old women who remembered more inspiring sermons when priests were not limited by the government.

My time as an altar boy was my last serious association with the Catholic Church. I was too proud and independent to need God, and there were too many other distractions like motorcycles, beer, and girls!

Map of Czechoslovakia with Nyrsko (lower southwest corner), Prague, and Ostrava

Chapter 3

By the time I was sixteen, I started to understand what real freedom meant—what we didn't have, free thinking, freedom to make our own choices, and to travel anywhere we wanted, not just to other Eastern Bloc countries.

By then, Czechoslovakia was heavily under Communism, and I realized what kind of social and political grip the government had on people.

I talked to my dad who had grown up in a free Bohemia until Germany invaded in 1939. He said, "You can have free thinking in your head and share it with your immediate family and true friends." Late at night he would listen to Radio Free Europe and Voice of America to hear the truth from the outside world. If others were listening also, no one knew. They didn't dare discuss it, for fear of repercussions. People who overheard you could betray you to the Communist authorities. Turning people in meant preferential treatment for them and rising in the ranks of the party.

My friends kept warning me that expressing my true feelings was risky. I grew more frustrated with the system and realized I couldn't live like that. For the first time, I played with the idea of living in another country, like maybe Germany. I started to hear reports of others doing this.

Many people made the difficult decision to try to escape from Czechoslovakia. In our town, where everyone knew each other, there were many strangers who came through on the way to the border. These tourists were all ages, singles and families from bigger towns like Pilsen or Prague.

Any town close to the German border, like Nyrsko, was closer to freedom than where they had come from. We had no way of knowing if they made it to freedom, if they had gotten caught and arrested, or had just disappeared.

There was a zone called *pohranicni pasmo* (border restricted zone) about a ten kilometer-wide area before the actual border. Only residents with proper permits proving they lived there were allowed in that area. Stories circulated about some people who lived in the zone who were actually helping a few escapees. Nobody knows how many they helped, or if they turned them in to the authorities.

We would have loved to have helped them as they came through Nyrsko, but we didn't dare. Although we secretly wished them success, we couldn't trust them. They could have been disguised agents, and we would have been arrested for helping them.

My friend's brother, who was a guard at the Zelezna Ruda border crossing to Germany, told me of one attempt. A man stole a heavy commercial truck and tried to force his way through the first gate. It was a fifteen centimeter (about six inches in diameter) metal pipe, which he broke through. He was being shot at, but he had a metal barrier raised in the bed of the truck that protected him. By the time he got to the main gate, which was an iron beam forty centimeters tall and twenty-six centimeters wide (about sixteen inches by ten), his truck was pretty much shot up, including the tires. But he was still rolling toward Germany and freedom.

This beam, which was designed to stop tanks, was as far as he got. Soldiers with machine guns caught up with him there and ended his attempt to escape. A half kilometer down the road, at the last crossing gate, German guards witnessed the massacre. Sadly, they could do nothing but watch. Later they verified this story to reporters for Radio Free Europe, and my dad also heard about it.

Immediately next to the borders, there were many ways to stop an escape. There were observation towers, touch-sensitive fences, walls, mine fields, barbed wire, miles of trenches, underground bunkers in some places, and automatic shooting mechanisms loaded with expanding bullets, as well as concrete and steel obstacles in all sizes and shapes. These things were designed to stop even a tank.

In my two years of military service, I remember walking fifty feet away from the border, on a marked path, with a loaded machine gun. I was scared to death, not so much of the danger from a possible German invasion, as we had been brainwashed into thinking, but from desperate Czechs who would do anything to escape.

There were stories of promotions in other military units for shooting escapees, but I don't think I could have shot my fellow countrymen. The German press loved to write escape stories, especially successful ones.

Radio Free Europe in Germany and Voice of America in West Chester, Ohio, had a free hand to broadcast escape attempts to those who could listen behind the Iron Curtain. There was heavy interference in the daytime, the least amount about two o'clock in the morning, when most people were sleeping.

Chapter 4

In most of Europe, students attend public school until age fourteen. Then they go to a trade school for three years. I studied metal technology to be a *klempner*, an auto body mechanic, in a town away from Nyrsko. We didn't just replace damaged parts on cars; we fixed or built them out of sheet metal, which was widely available.

For my graduation project, I designed and built a two-wheeled cycle with a body over it that I had seen in a magazine. It was entirely from metal and looked like a Dutch clog. It was powered by gears from an old bicycle, and the wheels were from an old wheelbarrow. I got a lot of compliments on it.

While I was at that school, I had the opportunity to learn to skydive. It was taught by a civil military club called Svazarm. They wanted to prepare students for military service, so we would be able to "fight the Americans when they invaded Czechoslovakia," we were told.

I forged my parents' signatures because I really wanted to do it but knew my folks would never give their permission. We had a lot of instruction about folding the square parachutes and we practiced that hundreds of times, knowing that lives depended on it being done precisely. We were petrified that if we didn't do it right, the chutes wouldn't open properly, and some jumper would slam into the ground and be killed.

After a few months, I finally got my chance to join the jumpers and got into the equipment. I was a small, skinny kid, and the gear was too big for me. I tightened the straps on the harness as far as they would go and puffed out my chest, but still they were loose on me—not too safe! My instructor told me to tighten them, so I turned around and pretended to adjust them.

Twenty of us guys went up in a Dakota plane, which was a copy of an old Lockheed model from World War II. Since the door opened to the outside, it had to be taken off, and we could see the ground fade away as we lifted off. I was exhilarated but mostly scared! When we got to 750 meters—about 2500 feet—the instructor hooked us on to the overhead cable. I was about in the middle of the jumping order and could see the terror and excitement on the faces of those ahead of me.

But the thrill of it far outweighed my fear. I took a big breath and jumped. Immediately my chute opened, and I was sitting on air, nothing underneath me. I had never experienced anything like that before. It lasted only a few fantastic minutes before I slammed into the ground. I ended up with a few bruises, especially on my thighs because of the loose harness; otherwise, I was unhurt. A truck picked us and our parachutes up and took us back to the hanger. Some guys couldn't wait to go up again—me being one—while others never wanted to go through that ordeal again!

I got to make three jumps, my last one on a day when my parents just happened to visit and learned what I was doing! My dad found out I had forged his signature and he immediately took me out of the program.

After graduation from the trade school, I worked in a local shop for two years until I was nineteen, then I was required to go into the military service. I did eighteen months of basic training in Stribro, which was on the main highway between Pilsen and Nuremberg Germany, through Rozvadov in northwest Bohemia.

Military watchtowers were at both sides of the highway by the base whose sole purpose was to spy on any car with a foreign license plate and record the type of vehicle, number of people in it, time of day, and which direction they were going. These were manned by Czech soldiers right up until the fall of Communism in 1989.

During our first trip back to Czechoslovakia as US citizens in 1977, we drove by these towers many times in a friend's car from Germany. They couldn't recognize many cars, especially if we drove fast. We smiled and waved at them as they followed us with their binoculars.

As a soldier, I was never selected to take part in this elite spying game. I was involved in a different service. Besides my assignment as a tow truck driver, I was in charge of overall fitness of my soldier-friends.

This stemmed from two soldiers drowning while crossing a river on maneuvers. My aim was for every soldier to be able to swim. Gymnastics, weight lifting, soccer, and ice hockey had all made me stronger and more athletic, and I wanted the same for the troops. I asked repeatedly for permission to teach swimming but was told there was no money, and no pool.

During one discussion, someone suggested I pursue it through membership in the Communist party, which I didn't take seriously, until then. Not knowing how difficult it would be in the future to escape from the party's grip, I joined with almost immediate results. Suddenly, a gym and pool became available. Once a week, I drove a truck packed with soldiers to Pilsen for swim lessons.

While the majority of them stayed with the program, it was an optional class. I wasn't their commanding officer, and I couldn't keep track of all of them all the time. Several dodged the class and went to a bar. When my superiors learned this, the swimming privilege was taken away.

It seemed that anything was possible, if it served the party's objectives. After a few months, in a small ceremony, I was awarded a certificate of achievement with a Russian *Pobeda* (victory) watch. Of course this practice of promoting zealous achievers for the Communist party followed me far into civilian life, despite my disillusionment with them.

I was constantly encouraged to continue my membership and follow up on my achievements in the service, but I was not interested. My motivation in joining had been only to make men and soldiers better all around, rather than climbing the ranks of the party.

A lot of people joined the Communist party to benefit their families. Membership meant preferential treatment in their kids' education, no matter what their grades were. Workers could get a paid day off for attending a rally, though most of them didn't believe in the propaganda either.

After my mandatory military service, I refused to take part in the meetings and activities with their false ideology and constant barrage of criticism of America and the West.

From my dad and his clandestine listening to the Voice of America and Radio Free Europe, I felt there had to be something more truthful and honest than what we were hearing from the Czech radio station.

Most older people had a simple radio with just an on/off knob. The clearest stations broadcasted Communist rhetoric and sometimes music.

In the military. Twenty years old.

Chapter 5

Another form of propaganda that couldn't be shut off was the system of loudspeakers. They were originally installed after 1948 at strategic locations in towns—on corner lampposts—so everyone could hear them broadcasting social and cultural events. They echoed against buildings, by the shops, at the town pool, and even the dead had no peace from them in the cemetery.

Under Communism they blared propaganda for half an hour at noon and at 5:00 p.m. when most people were leaving work. They touted inflated achievements of certain groups of workers, or some political nonsense, such as how much more steel was produced in Russia compared to American steel, which was used for weapons instead of hammers.

In one of the town squares, there was a huge statue of a steel worker hammering a sword into a plow. This was part of the propaganda, designed to show how peaceful and dedicated to hard work the Communist countries were, unlike the "war mongering" United States. In their stupidity, they actually depicted a scripture from the Bible: "They will beat their swords into plowshares" (Isaiah 2:4).

Food shortages were severe. People formed lines outside the grocery store before they opened in the morning and before they reopened after lunch. Even though there had been no shipments during the hour break, people lined up anyway, just in case. They waited for hours at the first rumor of a shipment, only to be disappointed when it never materialized. That scenario happened three times a week. People would stand in line for half an hour just to get a shopping cart in a store. The shelves were mostly empty, just breads, potatoes, flour for dumplings—a Czech staple—a few carrots, and dusty pyramids of canned meats or fish from Russia.

Sometimes we had cucumbers from a co-op many miles away. If people had gardens, they kept the harvest for themselves and friends. Milk was sold in plastic bags. Sometimes the cheap plastic would crack and leak, so they had to be sorted through to find one that didn't. When there were turnips, people would eat them the entire week. They made sauerkraut from them and ate that with some potatoes. Bananas and pineapple were available only at Christmastime and were a special treat. People did the best they could with the choices that were available, just concentrating on filling empty stomachs with sweet cakes, lots of potatoes, or dumplings.

Dumplings are boiled dough; some have pieces of old bread or potatoes added to the mix. They are shaped like a long cylinder, cooked, and sliced with thread into pieces the size of a hockey puck. A typical serving will have six or more dumplings on a plate with any one of many sauces. They still are a mainstay in Czech cooking today.

Small pieces of meat were served once or twice a week. I remember my mom being asked, "How many members in the family?" She was permitted to buy a set amount according to the number of family members. When Mom said her son was home for the weekend and she wanted to buy an additional portion of meat, it triggered a nasty response. "Anyone can say that." It was greasy food but filling and tasty.

We had chickens in a shed in our backyard so we always had fresh eggs and occasionally baked chicken. I had a noisy old pet rooster named Karl. He got nastier as he got older, chasing and attacking people until my dad said it was time for him to go. I chased him around the yard until I rounded him up and tried several times to stretch his neck on the chopping block. But he was too fast and pulled his head in, clawing me and drawing blood. I finally was faster than he was and lopped off his head. I lost my grip on him and in his final act of defiance, his headless body flew into a wall, leaving a trail of blood on the ground until he finally dropped and was on his way to becoming dinner.

There is a river in Nyrsko and occasionally I would go fishing with my friends for pike. My brother taught me how to kill them. He said to stick my thumb in the fishes' mouths and bend the heads back until the neck broke. This worked for most fish, but one time I caught one that wouldn't give in.

He had sharp teeth and when he started biting me I couldn't get my thumb out or break his neck. I finally did but not without some deep cuts on my thumb. By the time we grilled him over a camp fire, he had shrunk quite a bit. The pike tasted good and helped my throbbing thumb hurt a little less.

In the summer and fall, if the weather had been cool and wet, mushrooms would sprout in the woods. Many times I would go to a particular spot outside of town with my dad to look for them. He taught me which ones were safe to eat and which to avoid. He also jokingly warned me that some mushrooms were edible only once. We would fill our baskets and bring them home for my mother to slice and dry on newspaper in the sun. Then she would make them into a delicious sauce and serve them over dumplings. The dried mushrooms would keep all year long in the cold room.

Roads in Czechoslovakia were lined with apple and cherry trees. There were several kinds of cherries—small, big, sweet, tart—and many different apples. In the summer and fall, we would see cars pulled over and people with baskets picking the fruit to supplement their diets. Cherries found their way into pastries and wine, and apples became strudel, cakes, and spiked cider.

One December a semitruck fully loaded with oranges on the way from Turkey to Germany overturned about ten kilometers from the border. Four policemen were assigned to "guard" the spill overnight, until the replacement truck could arrive. Eyewitnesses recalled a lot of movement in the area that night and, lo and behold, in the morning when the truck arrived there was nothing left but orange juice!

The four cops swore to the investigators that the semi really had only been half full. The investigation went nowhere and the cops were freed from detention. But many families in Domazlice were specially blessed with exotic fruit at their Christmas table that year.

Once a year we would make our own sauerkraut. My parents would get a hundred heads of green and white cabbage from neighbors who had gardens. They weren't forbidden to grow things, but they were not permitted to sell them for a profit. Sometimes my dad would trade work for them.

We had a big ceramic barrel one meter tall (three feet) and three-quarters of a meter wide (two feet). Dad used a big stationary plane with many slanted steel blades in a wood frame. He would slide the heads back and forth cutting them into thin slices, which dropped onto a sheet below. My mother would scoop up the piles of slices and put them into the barrel, alternating layers of cabbage with salt, pepper, sliced onions, and garlic. My job was to stomp barefoot in the barrel to squeeze out the air and compress the layers. I would wash my feet thoroughly before and spend hours walking on the future sauerkraut. When the barrel was almost full, Dad would put the wood lid on top and heavy stones on top of the lid. The stones kept constant pressure on for the four months it took the cabbage to ferment in its own juice. The result: very white and tender feet for a few days, and wonderful sauerkraut for the whole winter. We often had meals of just dumplings and kraut—that was the best!

Stores didn't have shopping bags, so purchases were wrapped in paper or just carried in tote bags. Personal hygiene was difficult to maintain; soap and deodorant were expensive and people couldn't afford to use them. Oftentimes, dishes were washed in cold water only. Water was costly too, so people bathed infrequently.

I remember a friend's mom was working in a clothing store and she said clothes were made in Czechoslovakia, sent to Germany where labels were sewn in, and then exported back to my country as "German made." Often she would bring clothes home and trade them for food with neighbors who had gardens.

A friend working in a grocery told me they were shown how to market old bread as fresh. She was to step on the bag of bread just enough to loosen up the hard inside but not enough to break the crust. When customers squeezed it, it felt soft, so they bought it. But when they cut into it at home, the insides would all fall apart.

No one cared much for their teeth. There was little brushing, no flossing, and no calcium in their diets to strengthen them. Dental work was free and dentists would just pull teeth instead of trying to fix them when someone had a toothache. There was no preventive care, and most people lost teeth very young. Some got dentures—one size fits all. Painkillers were not widely used.

Medical care also was free, but people were afraid to go to doctors because so many who were sent to hospitals never returned. One of my friend's daughter spent two weeks in the hospital at five years old with an ear infection. She was isolated with other kids in an "infection unit," though they were not contagious. Visitation days were Wednesday and Sunday, and her parents could only view her from behind a glass partition. Hospital floors were constantly washed, but little else got such cleaning, and hand washing was just not important to them.

Czech beer and dumplings

Typical Czech holiday cookies

Chapter 6

Most people didn't drive and had no licenses for ID. Adults were, and are still, required to carry citizenship-proof books. They are about the size of a wallet and made of red plastic. Besides listing their name, address, and a picture, they also included names of parents and all employers. They are issued at age sixteen and are carried at all times, in case people are stopped and checked by the authorities. If we were between jobs, the authorities asked when we would be starting a new one. If an ID was lost, we had to report it immediately. Officials were concerned that it would be used for some illegal purpose, although I never heard of anything like that.

Officially there was no crime, even though prisons were full of people. Most were serving time for their political opinions, which were opposite the government.

My service in the military was six months short of two years, when I volunteered to work in the coal mines in Ostrava, a big industrial town in the eastern part of Czechoslovakia called Moravia. I knew it was going to be hard, physical work, but I was willing to take on that challenge in return for a salary that was three to four times higher than the average pay, because it was so dangerous.

There was a severe shortage of workers and a high demand for coal. Most homes and businesses used coal for heat and hot water.

I extended my three-year contract to six years and was able to help out my parents, as well as get things I wanted, like a motorcycle and nice clothes.

Conditions were brutal. The ceiling in the mines was about three-and-a-half-feet tall—a little more than a meter—so we were bent over for eight-hour shifts. It was very hard on the back and legs. It was very cold and I breathed fumes all day from the bedrock as we dug into it. And the equipment was very loud.

While in Moravia, we heard rumors of a store called Tuzex. It sold foreign-made goods like clothes, Swiss Army knives, liquor, appliances, cigarettes, and even cars. The stores were designed for tourists, accepting only "bons," which had been exchanged for hard currency like the Deutsche mark, dollar, and British pound. The average Czech couldn't afford to shop there. Family outside the country could send in money or they could exchange their Koruna for bons at a very high rate.

At that time, there were about forty Tuzex stores in the country. When I was in Ostrava, making good money, I traded for bons and got to shop there. I was like a kid in a candy store, seeing all these goods from exotic foreign lands.

I bought my first Rider jeans for a week's pay. Real ones with tags and rivets! I framed and hung the garment tags on my wall for my friends to admire. Those jeans lasted years. My country tried to make jeans, but they were worse than work clothes, awful fabric, not denim, and badly fitting.

Later, when I lived in New York City, I was able to shop from a Tuzex catalog and send my family pretty packages. At Christmas, I sent them chocolates, cigarettes, liquor, soap, coffee, hand cream, and specialty foods. It was such a special treat for them.

I bought cars for my brother and sisters through the Tuzex catalog also. The Fiat 128 that I purchased for my brother cost about $2000 in 1975.

Chapter 7

Motorcycles and cars were my passion, and my first motorbike was a Norton that I bought from the son of a British attaché. I had a lot of fun with it and later I exchanged it for an eight-year-old Fiat 600.

I did all my own repairs on that car. My friend Ludvik and I would work on our cars in a park area by the river in front of his house. We spent a lot of time keeping the engines spotless and the exterior polished. We drew a lot of attention from guys interested in cars and girls interested in us.

I was envied because I worked hard to get my own car and had not come from a wealthy family. The greatest benefit was the independence that a car brought me. I drove my parents to festivals and shopping places they could never have visited on their own.

When my contract in the mines expired in 1967, I returned to Nyrsko and started working in Okula in the maintenance department. Okula had a long tradition of manufacturing optical lenses, dating back to the late 1800s. Since their quality was not up to Western standards, 80 percent of the lenses were exported to other Eastern Bloc-Iron Curtain countries, mainly Russia.

These lenses were used in eyeglasses, telescopes, and binoculars. In the early 1900s, another Okula factory had been built at the opposite end of town that made eyeglass frames, deflector shields for motorbikes, and an ever-expanding range of products. Okula became the main manufacturer of glass and plastic products in Czechoslovakia.

I did various tasks in the maintenance department, mostly keeping the machinery in good working order. Oftentimes we had to design and build our own equipment, because it wasn't available in our limited socialist markets.

Bohemia, as the country had been called during the Hapsburg Austrian monarchy until 1918, had been one of the richest and most technologically advanced countries in Europe. Under Communism, it had been reduced to a destitute satellite country, hopeless and broken in spirit. I was full of rage!

Chapter 8

In early 1968, Prague Spring happened. It was a peaceful turnover from the rigid Communist rule to a more moderate Communist system of democracy.

Alexander Dubcek was nominated as the party secretary. His position was more powerful than President Novotny, who was subsequently replaced by President Svoboda. His name means "liberty" in Czech.

There were social changes in the country, and it felt like the rebirth of our nation. We were all filled with great joy and optimism for a better life and a future full of hope, freedom, and independence.

Limited ownership of land and businesses was allowed, and some adventurous people were willing to take the risk. The draw of owning and controlling their own enterprise was irresistible.

The borders were open and people were free to travel. Some walked across the border to Germany to ogle shop windows and admire the beautiful towns. They couldn't buy anything, but it was so exciting to see what was available in the outside world. Others who had families or connections in countries like England or Austria could freely visit them.

There was freedom of speech without fear of reprisal. Newspapers had fewer restrictions and voiced people's real opinions. My friends and I talked endlessly about new possibilities without fear of being spied on by people sympathetic to the old regime. We had great expectations for the kinds of freedoms that America enjoys every day.

But Dubcek's "Communism with a human face," as it was called, didn't go over well with the hardcore members of the party who wanted to maintain their grip. They let him make some changes because they thought it was only temporary. They were aware of the danger of such a movement. It could lead to rebellion, and it was closely monitored and disliked by the Russian leadership, who couldn't afford to lose the most prosperous country in the Eastern Bloc.

They were calling it a Western conspiracy, despite the fact that America and the West had absolutely nothing to do with it. It was also labeled a "Contra Revolution" by the Kremlin.

Those few months were taken for granted by all of us. We had no idea that an even greater conspiracy was being conceived by former leaders and the Soviet Union.

The invasion on August 20, 1968, was a shock to all. It felt like a death sentence. The official statement was that Czech leaders had "invited" Warsaw Pact armies to crush the Contra Revolution, which was supposedly taking place, though everyone knew that it was Russia that decided to disrupt the peaceful movement.

On that morning, my country was invaded by tanks and military personnel of the Warsaw Pact countries. Border crossings were secured, and no one could leave or enter Czechoslovakia. I remember hearing about the invasion at 6 a.m. on my way to work. People were advised to stay calm and not provoke the soldiers who came to "rescue" us. I don't think any work got done that day; everyone was huddled around radios keeping up with all the news.

In Prague, protesters were throwing rocks and blocking streets with cars. They were demanding an explanation from the Russian soldiers asking, "Why, why, you're supposed to be our brothers?" There was some shooting in Wenceslav Square by the National Museum, breaking windows and leaving scars on the facade.

A few people were killed and wounded. A student named Jan Palach burned himself to death in the square to protest the occupation and the hopelessness of the situation. We watched trucks full of soldiers drive through our town of Nyrsko, on the way to "secure the borders." The truth was so they could prevent people from leaving the country. Road signs were turned around to confuse the invaders. Most of us were standing in total disbelief and shock, shaking our fists. I was sure that any act of aggression toward them would have been answered with their Kalishnikov machine guns.

These soldiers were unshaved, dirty, with ill-fitting uniforms, not regular troops. Possibly their leaders had expected strong opposition from the Czechs and sent this first wave of soldiers as a sacrifice.

Their faces were expressionless.

The soldiers took over the local and national newspapers, the railroad stations, and city halls in Nyrsko and other towns. They were stationed in bases throughout the country, as an occupying force. One base was in the next town over from ours.

In the fall of 1968, Dubcek, the secretary of the Communist party, was detained and President Svoboda was replaced by the pro-Russian premier Husak and his cronies. The situation felt desperate. The beautiful dream of freedom seemed lost forever as the grip of the Communist Party tightened even more.

Chapter 9

Life again seemed hopeless. For the first time, I was seriously considering leaving my country and family. But after talking about it over a beer with friends, the reality of abandoning everything—my family, my possessions—sank in. I knew that if I actually did make it, I could never return to this familiar life and my hometown.

My girlfriend, Anna, and I had discussed leaving many times. The plan was for me to go first, and she would follow me later, once I got established. We hoped to get married and start over together in the free world. She gave me two books about life and travel to different countries, which I carried with me at all times.

The excitement that I felt just talking about it and imagining all the possibilities in the West overshadowed the uncertainty of such a move and what was actually involved in leaving. So many unknowns. The arguments for and against going were ever present. I knew I had to go, but leaving my familiar life and family forever was a very scary thought.

With every month that passed, time worked against me. I was twenty-five and knew it wouldn't get easier. Having all my life ahead of me, I didn't want to start over at middle age.

Nothing was improving. Things were getting worse, and it was more and more difficult to stay quiet and not express my opinions. People were becoming more passive and accepting the situation. They were depressed, disappointed, and frustrated; the worst part was that no one could do anything about it.

I told my dad several times, "This system will never change," and I truly believed it.

But he said, "Given time it will," which I never accepted at that time.

Of course he was right, as usual, and I would have been very happy to admit to him that I was wrong, but he passed away in May 1989, five months before the Velvet Revolution.

Escaping the Iron Curtain

Chapter 10

I decided to try to escape. Then the endless planning and reconsidering started. Trips to West Germany were allowed by personal invitation only—if the person living there pledged to fully support you. So a friend of my sister living in West Germany invited me and two friends.

It was the summer of 1969. It didn't seem too scary because we were only going to the country next door, not too far from Nyrsko. I packed a few clothes, the books from Anna, several cans of meat, crackers, along with Czech money and my passport. Before World War II, people had been able to work in nearby countries like Austria and Germany. Because of that, my parents were not too concerned. They said, "Go, give it a try." Anna was sad and secretly hoping, as were my brother and others, that I would be back in a few days.

One of my friends was reluctant to go. Knowing that strength was in numbers, on the departure date we "helped" him pack his suitcase by throwing everything into it for him and dragging him to the station with us. After a three-hour train ride to Furth by Nurnberg, Germany, we arrived at Hubert's apartment. He gave us beer and snacks, then drove us to a refugee camp at Zirndorf, a half hour away.

There were appalling conditions—kids and dogs running loose, and it was smelly and trashy. Hubert spoke to the guards for us and walked around the camp with us. There were mostly Czechs, but also Polish, Albanian, and Romanian. For some of them it was probably better than what they had had at home; for us it was discouraging and a letdown. I don't know what we expected, but not this. We decided not to stay in the camp.

At one point, Hubert had told me that if it had been just me, he would have let me stay at his place, but the three of us in his little apartment with his family was impossible .

So he left us at the town square in Furth where many other escapees were camping. Obviously, we were not the only ones who felt disappointed by the refugee camp and had decided not to stay there. We did not believe that the starting point of our new free lives was supposed to look like that.

We stayed in the town for two days and nights, eating our own limited supplies, drinking from the city fountain, wandering endlessly around town, and gazing at store windows with beautiful things and clean streets. It was degrading. Finally we thought, *What are we doing here?* The German people mostly ignored us, and they seemed disgusted with us for disrupting their lives.

I couldn't stop thinking of the great paradox between the locals with bags of groceries going to their beautiful comfortable homes and us, the homeless living in the square. I knew the great free life had to have humble beginnings, but this was discouraging. Most people probably returned to their countries after this disappointing introduction to West Germany. But what did we all expect? Starting over in a strange country with no job, no money, and no language—it was going to be much harder than we could possibly have imagined.

Chapter 11

Discussions about our great escape kept running through our minds. It had been so much easier to just talk about escaping over several beers back home, than actually doing it. Suddenly, our country didn't seem so bad after all. We had work, girls, friends, and a place to live.

It crossed my mind that if my two friends had not been with me, I would have stayed in Germany and tried to make it on my own. But God had other plans for me. Part of it was a stranger from Slovakia who approached us in the park in Furth and asked if any of us could drive. He had bought a second car in Germany and needed someone to drive it back to his home in Slovakia. We were to follow him home, and since I was the only one who had a driver's license, we had an easy way to return home.

Suddenly, the question of how we all would get back home was resolved. I dropped my two friends off in Nyrsko on our way through before continuing on. After a twenty-hour drive through Germany, Bohemia, Moravia, and Slovakia, we finally reached his home. He paid me generously, and I took a train to Moravia, stopping to see my sister for a few days, before heading back home to Nyrsko. I thought, *There is always another time to try to escape.*

The year was 1970. Back in Nyrsko, we started new escape plans. This time we would go through Egypt in April, before it got really hot there. We were permitted to travel there because it was Russian friendly at that time, and there were no other countries except for Libya to escape to from there.

After a year of planning, two friends and I had finally saved enough money. We booked a trip to Alexandria, Egypt. This was our first time on a commercial flight, and it was a whole new experience. The takeoff, landing, and food service made us feel very special. The vision of being able to fly anywhere in the world someday was exciting and scary at the same time. The world looked so beautiful from that altitude and the possibilities seemed endless.

The major decisions that we faced about our planned escape in the next few days did not take away from the excitement we felt at that moment. They seemed so far away.

As I descended the stairs from the plane in the early evening, a warm, tropical breeze brushed against my face, and I felt incredibly happy to be alive.

There was an established beachfront community where Czech currency was accepted and our language was spoken by some Egyptians— hotel staff, kids, and especially the beach vendors. We enjoyed a few days of carefree living, good food, and the warm Mediterranean ocean.

But in the back of our minds was always the thought that we were not going back and would try to stay. We had to go to Cairo to secure visa extensions, so we could work in the country and hopefully make enough money to travel to the United States.

It was several hours away by cab to the Czech embassy where we met with the friendly ambassador who thankfully was willing to extend our visas. He advised us more like a father than a state official. The job market in Egypt was bad, and work permits for foreigners were almost impossible to obtain.

We could see beautiful villas being built next to the embassy, and the architecture was astounding. I commented about the scrawny men building them—carrying baskets of mortar on their heads up the scaffolding. It reminded me of ants climbing an ant hill. I commented that I could carry two or three times as much on one trip, since I was in excellent physical condition.

But according to the ambassador, any foreign workers, if they were hired, were in danger from the locals trying to protect their livelihood. Also the compensation was below even eastern European standards. The average worker was making twenty-eight *piastras* a day—the price of two packs of cigarettes—and we were all smokers.

Besides discrimination from the fellow workers, we faced another danger. We asked the ambassador about the chances for work in neighboring Libya. He informed us about shootings at the border between the two countries. Many recent college graduates in Egypt could not find work in their home country and were running across the border. There were more work opportunities in Libya, especially in the gas refineries. They were being shot at by Egyptian guards and patrols trying to stop them, a situation similar to what we had just left in Czechoslovakia!

In light of this fact, we couldn't have gotten there legally or safely. So the dilemma looming over our heads was the same: either be shot at the Egypt–Libya border or back home at the Czech–German border. What a choice! I was willing to take a chance and hopefully beat the odds, but my other two friends were not. If you're dead, there is no hope for anything, which I reluctantly agreed with.

I had conflicting emotions—dashed hopes for an escape through Egypt but comfortable feelings of returning to our familiar life again. I harbored hope for another attempt in the future.

Chapter 12

After ten days in Egypt, we decided to return to Czechoslovakia and try again later, thinking the third time must be the charm.

Within four months, we booked a three-day trip to Austria where, we thought, the Traiskirchen refugee camp south of Vienna would be a good place to start. Two weeks before our departure, the travel agency Cedok called and informed us that the Czech government had cancelled all trips shorter than a week to any capitalist country, including Austria. They obviously had caught on that people were defecting while on these short excursions.

There was a big red cancellation stamp across the Austrian visa in my passport. So that same day we booked a two-week trip to Sibenik, Yugoslavia—plan four! In 1970 Yugoslavia, under President Tito was Communist, but very western friendly, which we thought would be better than Egypt under President Nasser who was pro-Russian.

This time, only my friend Petr and his wife, Klara, were going to try to escape with me. We booked a stay at a resort with full pension so meals were provided. I took my suitcase this time and besides a few clothes and the books from Anna, I put in eight cans of meat to eat during the escape. There was no turning back for me.

We flew there and spent two glorious weeks on Sibenik beaches, soaking up the sun and ocean, enjoying the food and night life. We fantasized about what life might be like in whatever country we ended up. We were dreaming of Germany, Austria, Switzerland, or America.

Map of Italy with Trieste, Bari, and Capua

Chapter 13

Inevitably, the last day of our stay came, and the decision to escape or not had to be made that evening. We talked until two in the morning with no resolution.

The emotional scene has been embedded in my mind forever. Klara was crying inconsolably and arguing that she could not leave her elderly mother in Czechoslovakia. It would have felt so comfortable to say, "Okay let's try later," but I knew that if I didn't escape this time I might not get another chance. Government regulations and borders were getting even tighter.

What made it even worse was the uncertainty of our future—what to expect. Petr and Klara at least sort of knew what they were going to face when they returned to Czechoslovakia: questioning, confiscated passports, forbidden travel, job loss or jail, or all of the above. For me, only God knew what lay in my future.

Petr finally agreed to return with his wife. One of the hardest times in my life was saying good-bye to them, not knowing when or if I would ever see them again.

As we said our emotional good-byes, Petr handed me a dollar that he had been saving for our escape and said, "You need this more than I." I carried that bill in my wallet for years as a reminder of that night.

Interestingly, Sibenik in Czech means "town of gallows" and that was to be the beginning point of my journey to freedom. What a place to start. At 3:00 a.m., with no buses available at that time of night, I called a cab. The thirty-minute ride to the train station was uneventful until I got there and the driver requested an exorbitant fare, which would have taken most of my money. I knew I was grossly overcharged, but there was nothing I could do. He had figured out that I was attempting to escape, and he had locked my suitcase in the trunk.

He threatened to call the police, which I couldn't risk. I was so angry and felt so helpless, but I couldn't succumb to it or my great attempt for freedom may have ended that night, right there. So I paid him what he demanded and boarded the five o'clock train to Ljubliana.

Two hours later, in the early morning, I wandered the streets dragging my suitcase, asking people where the embassies were.

There were a lot of travelers at that time, just not many who were traveling by foot. I was exhausted and very discouraged. I had little money and just short of begging there were no options available.

I found the German embassy first; they were very friendly and I asked for a work visa, "Ich will in deutchland arbeiten," but they said they weren't issuing work visas at the time, because the job market was overcrowded with so many escapees. So I left and went to the Swiss embassy—the same result.

By this time, I was sick and tired of begging any western country in Europe to take me in. I was especially angry because I had a clean record back home, I did not owe any money to anybody, and I did not have a criminal history. Later on I learned, from my parents, that I had been sentenced for illegally staying abroad. If I had returned, I would have been jailed or at least prevented from traveling anywhere again.

I knew I had to get out of Yugoslavia because I could have been arrested and deported at any time for staying past my date of return. My travel papers allowed me to stay in the resort only. By not flying back home on that day, I forfeited my airline ticket. And I am sure the Czech government was immediately notified of my escape.

The embassies were in different parts of the city and by the time I got to the Austrian one, it was late afternoon. At the embassy, I hoped they wouldn't understand the cancellation stamp over the Austrian visa in my passport. In broken German I kept requesting a permit to work there. It was a comical scene, as they attempted to figure out what *"neplatne"* meant. I desperately tried to convince them that the big red mark was a mistake by the Czech clerk and meant nothing of importance.

The deadlock was resolved when they found a staff worker who understood Czech and translated it. They refused to issue me a work visa.

It raced through my mind how easily my life could have been changed, if they had said yes to my request. I was desperate! This was my last hope; I could not take no for an answer. But they opened the door for me and politely requested that I leave.

With hatred for the entire German world, I decided right there not to emigrate anywhere where German was spoken. By then, it was about 4:00 p.m. in the afternoon, and I went to the park.

Thankfully, I still had canned meat and I drank water from the fountain in the middle of the park as I studied the country map to figure out what my next move might be.

Chapter 14

My only choice from there was to head for Italy, the closest country that was accepting political refugees. Though hitchhiking would save me money, it was more dangerous, so I decided to take the train.

I had only enough money to get to the town, which was fifteen kilometers before the border, but I stayed on the train past my stop, carefully eluding the conductor, dragging my suitcase around, hiding in the bathroom. Eventually he did find me and threw me off the train at the next stop. I was thankful he didn't report me to the authorities.

It was ten o'clock at night when I started walking on the railroad tracks toward Italy and freedom. I followed a map, which showed the railroad tracks clearly heading out of Yugoslavia.

Two trains passed me that night, but they were going too fast for me to consider jumping on, and I had to run into the bushes for safety. I was in a tunnel when the second one came through, barely missing me. Behind the windows, the passengers seemed so worry free. How I envied them.

I almost walked into a border patrol that was warming themselves by a campfire. They were guarding the border against tobacco and alcohol smugglers. I left the tracks and made a wide circle, perhaps eight to ten kilometers, around the guards.

By partial moonlight, I went from the relatively flat ground beside the tracks to bushes, deep ravines, and uneven terrain. At one point, I had to climb a huge rock. As I sat perched like a bird on top, I momentarily felt incredible joy to be alive. The air was cool and fresh, some stars were twinkling overhead, and I inhaled deeply, taking in the wonder of it all. Under any other circumstances I would have let out a shout.

I was heading toward freedom and my destiny. I was excited and scared at the same time.

Not knowing how far the border soldiers were, I had to be very quiet. I hadn't eaten much for most of the day and I was pretty hungry. But I ignored my stomach and pressed on; I wanted to be in Italy by daylight.

All of my senses were magnified. My eyes strained to find a way through the brush, carefully avoiding branches or anything that would make noise and give me away. My clothes were being snagged and torn by branches, but I did not care; I had to keep going. I heard animals scampering about in the dark, but the loudest noise was my own heart pounding in my chest.

At some point, I came across some paper debris with Italian writing on it. Just about when I was ready to jump for joy and dance, thinking I was in Italy, suddenly I broke out in a cold sweat realizing that the paper could have been carried over with the wind from Italy and I still might be in Yugoslavia. So I kept quiet and continued on.

It was in the early dawn that I came upon a clearing that looked like a town disposal site. I saw milk cartons with *lecce* (Italian for "milk") on it. I was finally convinced I was in Italy and then I let out a joyful scream! With a burst of adrenalin, I had new energy to keep walking.

In the brightening daylight, I continued to follow a dirt road that became paved. Heading west, with the sun warming my back, cars and trucks with Italian license plates drove by. I was ecstatic!

I must have been a sight, stumbling down the road, in torn clothes, and hauling a beat-up suitcase, but my heart was overjoyed. I was hoping that the worst part of my journey was finally behind me.

The road zigzagged down to the ocean port city of Trieste. I passed several buildings and barracks that resembled a concentration camp from World War II. Later on, I discovered that this was the very same refugee camp that I was to be taken to.

Chapter 15

I reached the port city by early morning and was completely exhausted, having just walked through the longest night of my life. I found a park where other homeless people were sleeping under the trees. The last thing I remember was using the belt from my pants to tie my suitcase to my arm, so it would not get stolen, before I fell into a deep sleep.

About ten or eleven hours later, I woke up quite hungry and ate two cans of lunch meat from my suitcase. Another homeless man was staring at me, obviously hungry too, so I shared it with him. I knew only a few words of Italian so I spoke to him in broken German and Czech, but mostly sign language. Sharing my food helped a lot in communicating with him.

Finally, I felt safe enough to tell somebody I was running away from Communism. For a brief moment, there was a certain attraction to his kind of life—free to go wherever he wanted, without responsibility, but also without any kind of future. I wasn't risking my life for just that; I wanted more, much more.

By late afternoon, some of the men in the park started to drink. I knew it was time for me to go to the police to ask for political asylum, which was my only option. So I picked up my suitcase and walked until I found a police station.

The Carabinieri at the station took my Czech passport and sent me to the waiting room, where there were at least a dozen people from Albania, Romania, Hungary, and Poland. In the evening, after endless waiting, we were herded onto a bus and driven about eight kilometers to the refugee camp.

To my horror, we were headed back on the same winding road toward the Yugoslavian border that I had just walked down earlier that day! In a panic, I thought about jumping off the bus if we kept going, but before I could do that we turned into the barracks that I had passed that morning.

It was packed with three to four hundred people from all over Europe. It had been a concentration camp in World War II, and there was plenty of evidence—like shrapnel marks on the walls and broken windows.

I was assigned a bottom bunk bed in a room with twenty other people mostly from Poland and Turkey. In my month there, I met only one Czech family who had escaped from a sightseeing boat in Venice.

We got three meals a day and waited to be processed. The officials in charge of the camp checked our backgrounds to see if we had a criminal history in our home countries. Some people were actually deported. I was transferred to the southern Italian town of Capua near Naples. There I stayed for six months.

Chapter 16

It was another concentration camp from Mussolini's era. The American Red Cross mostly financed the operation of it, providing food, clothing, and the processing of refugees. There were endless background checks and nothing seemed to be moving forward, maybe because it was summer vacation time.

Communication was always a problem so I tried to learn some Italian. There were job offers outside the camp and I took one nearby, working in a gas station pumping gas, washing windshields, and doing any necessary chores.

Despite the three thousand lira a day pay—a few dollars—I really enjoyed the variety of cars. They were all big and beautiful to me. I offered to check the oil just so I could open the hoods and see the engines! I dreamed about owning one of them in the future.

Customers were mostly friendly and appreciated the extra free service; some even tipped me! The boss was very happy too and offered to facilitate my papers if I stayed to work for him.

But a few months later, someone offered me a job in a sandpit for four thousand lire a day. They were extracting sand from the river and they needed someone to weld the teeth on the buckets that had been broken from dredging the bottom. I had learned welding in school back home and I enjoyed it.

Two months later, I joined a couple of Czech friends whom I had met in the camp, who were working in town, loading and unloading heavy cow hides in a tannery. They were big and stiff as boards and saturated with salt. It was the same pay, but a lot more fun and good physical exercise.

Twice, a friend and I hitchhiked across the peninsula to the east coast, to a blood center in Bari to sell our blood. It took about six hours each way and paid us eight thousand lira, twice what our jobs paid us. We spent some of the money on pizza on the way back to the camp.

Another time, three of us took a ferry ride to the island of Capri. The sea was rough and we all got sick on the boat. When we got to the shore, and our stomachs finally calmed down, we had a great time. I enjoyed the beach until I stepped on a sea urchin and let out a few expletives in Czech.

To my surprise, a young lady came up to me and said in my language, "You know, some people can understand you." She helped me pull the stingers out of my foot and then invited us three to have dinner with her and her father; they were vacationing on the island.

The restaurant they took us to overlooked the beach, and the sunset from there was spectacular. We spent several hours feasting and sharing our stories. It was so easy to forget our circumstances and imagine ourselves in a life such as they had. We enjoyed many courses of rich food and learned her dad had been an aerial acrobat pilot in Czechoslovakia. During one of his shows, he just kept on flying and never went back! Now he was a private pilot for an Italian count who was the owner of MV Agusta, a motorcycle company.

Eventually, we had to get back to the reality of being political refugees living in a camp. We thanked them for their generosity and headed back to the camp late at night. Thankfully the ocean was calm on the return trip.

Letters from my family and my girlfriend, Anna, gave me courage. Mail was opened and read by the Communists before it left the country, but I still heard about some repercussions that my family suffered because of my escape. Even though I had sold my car to my sister and she had a bill of sale, it was confiscated. My parents were questioned and my clothes were taken from their house. Anna still sounded like she planned on joining me later, though I was beginning to doubt her.

Some refugees grew tired of the slow pace of processing and the deteriorating conditions in the camp—loose dogs, disorderly people, general filth. Some friends chose to leave and take a train to Germany where they had connections and guaranteed work. But most of us decided to go through the grueling process of filling out questionnaires and deciding what countries might be in our futures . . . and waiting.

As for me, I had firmly decided not to stay in Europe. My disappointing experiences in the Swiss, Austrian, and German embassies still weighed heavily on my mind. People were applying to go to Australia, South Africa, and America. They told us that's where the most jobs were available.

Chapter 17

My heart was set on America. Years ago, my pro-Western science teacher in Czechoslovakia was calling it a "science laboratory of mankind." Later I learned that that teacher had lost his job because of his pro-Western views.

Finally after six months, I was called in to be interviewed by the American attaché in Naples. I heard rumors about these interviews, and the biggest obstacle for granting entry to the United States was trying to conceal membership in the Communist Party back home. I knew personally of one Czech from Prague who was denied entry to the States because he tried to hide his membership and it was found out.

I had filled out my forms honestly and admitted my involvement in the party, offering to further explain my reasons why I had been. When my interview finally took place, it was through a Russian translator.

What a paradox. I was concerned about his honesty and accurately translating what I had to say. At one point, I asked the attaché if he personally would ever join the Communist Party. He said no. I was trying to make the point that I was someone who had already been a member and knew of their deceptive policies, versus someone who hadn't experienced it. I emphatically told him, "Even if my life depended on it, I would absolutely never again be associated with the Communist Party."

The next two weeks felt like an eternity as I waited to hear if I'd been accepted. I second-guessed everything I had said. For the first time, I realized I was not in control, that my fate was in the hands of a greater power.

I continued taking English lessons in a class that had shrunk from thirty to three pupils by the third week. Our teacher from Scotland spoke only English, which had discouraged most of the other students. The dropouts thought they would learn English twice as fast once they got to America. I was thrilled to learn as much as possible and looked forward to the two hours a week of English. Besides it being pleasant to listen to, I knew it would be useful to know a few words in my new country when looking for a job.

When I was finally called to the *guestura* office, my heart was in my throat. To my great joy, I learned I was going to America! Hallelujah! My dream was about to come true! I was issued an Italian refugee passport and visa for America.

They gave me clothes, which had been provided by the American Red Cross. These were ugly and ill fitting, and I promptly threw them over the fence to gypsy families who were camping on the other side. These families lived outside the camp and some even had cars. But they knew refugees moved in and out, and many of them left belongings behind.

I wanted to look really good for my new country, so I went shopping. In the department store, Standa, I bought myself a winter coat, sweater, shoes, and a better suitcase. My old one was battle scarred from crossing the mountain range during my escape, and it got tossed over the fence too.

My arrival in New York City 1970

New Beginnings

Chapter 18

Several of my Czech friends were also going to America. They had escaped Czechoslovakia by taking a boat ride to Italy and staying ashore. We were bussed from the camp to the airport in Rome.

I learned the US Catholic Conference paid for my airline ticket to New York City on TWA. They told me, "If you repay us, we can help others in their quest for freedom." Most people did not repay them, but I did with my first paychecks. The clerk at the USCC office commented that I was the first from my group to do so. It made me feel honored and proud.

The flight originated in the Middle East and was full of refugees from that region. I was appalled to see how badly they behaved—unsupervised kids ran up and down the aisles tearing up paper bags, screaming, and bothering people. With the noise that was coming from their section of the plane, I half expected to see chickens or pigs too.

The flight felt endless, but I had high hopes that I would be treated with great respect when I arrived, rather than as just another refugee like them, since I had new clothes on and felt very special about coming to America.

But there was no big welcome; nobody noticed. After going through customs and immigration, we were herded onto a bus and taken to the hotel Wollcott in lower Manhattan. It was a homeless shelter, and there was no welcoming committee there either, just a beggar outside asking for money. I was very disappointed to come to my new country and have an encounter like that. I had expected a much different introduction.

I had six roommates and shared a bathroom down the hall with twenty other guys, mostly from Poland. The conditions were not much better than in the Italian camp, and I overheard them praising Italy over

New York often saying, "Italia bella," wishing they had not left. But no one could have known what it would be like here.

I was determined to move to my own place as soon as I found work. Several businesses in New York placed wanted ads in the hallway, and I answered one for a painter. My boss was from Yugoslavia, and I had mixed feelings about working for him. I remembered his fellow countryman—the taxi driver who had robbed me a few months ago.

But three days after arriving in New York City, I was working. My first job was painting and fixing walls in a two-story penthouse apartment of a high-rise overlooking the East River. It belonged to Mayor John Lindsay's sister. I used my experience from repairing my dad's house back home.

My boss liked my work and two weeks later he offered me an apartment near him in the Bronx. He owned the building and did not charge me rent! It was a furnished basement flat. A week later I invited two Czech friends, who weren't working yet, to share it with me. That location made it much easier for my boss to pick me up for work.

The three of us spent hours in the evenings on the pedestrian bridge over the Deegan Expressway watching the traffic. We were amazed at the volume of cars on this six-lane road and loved guessing what type of vehicles they were. It renewed my old passion for cars and inspired me to look for a job related to them.

On weekends, while my roommates were watching TV, I visited auto shops, garages, and gas stations. Most of them wanted mechanics with experience and tools, and I had neither. My search for such a job took quite a while.

Chapter 19

One day I walked into Spuyten Duyvil auto wreckers in Upper Manhattan. With my heavy accent I said, "I'm looking for a job." An elderly man approached me with distrust in his eyes. He told me there were no openings.

However, as I turned to go, his son stepped in and offered me a job as a welder and driver in the salvage yard. He would pay me $1.80 an hour. It was 1971 and most likely below the minimum wage, but the smell of car grease and oil was priceless to me, and I would have gladly taken the job for even less money.

Feeling slightly guilty about taking another job, I arranged for one of my roommates to take my place painting, so we could keep the apartment. A few days later, I was doing whatever service was needed, mounting tires for customers, doing tune-ups, and welding mufflers.

I also cut out the engines and gas tanks from vehicles destined for the crusher. There would be three cars stacked up and chained to the truck, which I drove twenty minutes across town, a couple of times a week. That was the most fun for me, because now I was part of the traffic that I used to just watch go by.

One ride was quite memorable and pretty scary. Without me knowing, the hood on the top car became unlatched and flew open. The next thing I heard was a horrible crash, metal on metal. The hood had been sheared off going under an overpass. In my side-view mirror, I watched helplessly as it somersaulted down the highway and cars swerved to avoid it. I envisioned it beheading people in the cars behind me. It wasn't possible for me to stop and retrieve it; it was quite a spectacle. Under any other circumstances, I would have laughed. For the first time in my life I prayed no one would be hurt. On my return trip I spotted the hood, flattened like a pancake, in the breakdown lane.

Following that incident, and jokes from my coworkers, I made sure the top hood was always chained securely to the chassis after that.

My duties also included driving a Volkswagen, which had been converted to a dune buggy, to get lunches for my coworkers. I was stopped several times by cops, and, since I didn't have a New York driver's license yet, I showed them my Czech one. Of course they couldn't read it, but they understood and never gave me a ticket.

I knew I had to get my license eventually, but I was apprehensive about taking the chauffeur's license exam because of my limited English. Finally, eight months after starting this job, I took the test, praying I could understand the questions and multiple-choice answers. At one point, I asked the instructor to clarify a question, but he misunderstood me, thinking I was asking him for an answer. I was almost thrown out of the class.

I struggled through and passed by one point. When I returned to the shop, what a celebration party they had for me, complete with champagne and snacks! It was a mystery to me how they could have been so sure I would pass. I was glad to finally have the correct papers to be a licensed truck driver in the United States.

Since the subway stops were not convenient to my apartment, I walked to and from my job in the Bronx, about five miles round trip. Besides, I enjoyed watching the traffic. There were so many makes of cars—that I could only dream about—and I knew one day I would be driving my own.

My boss's father gave me rides once in a while, and when he suggested that the company could help me get a car I was absolutely thrilled!

There was a 1960 Ford Falcon available for $100, but I wanted a 1964 Buick Special. It was $200 more, but it was beautiful and I loved it.

With my new Buick, I made many trips with my friends to upstate New York and the surrounding areas. My first big adventure was a trip to Florida's Miami Beach before Christmas, about a two thousand-kilometer (1243 miles) drive, with four Czech friends.

I filled up two discarded gas tanks from the old vehicles in the yard and carried them in the trunk along with our bags. We were all smokers and we had to be very careful. What a fire hazard we were! It was like driving with a bomb in our trunk! Along the way we used up the gas from the spare tanks and discarded them. This extra fuel got us all the way to Georgia. At that time, gas was only $.30 a gallon, but it helped not having to buy it until then.

The further south we drove the warmer the air became, and we were caught up in the thrill of the tropics. Passing acres of orange groves was incredible. The sweet smell was intoxicating! We shed our winter clothes and stripped down to shorts and t-shirts in December. It felt fantastic!

Warm rain greeted us in the early morning hours as we crossed the causeway to Miami Beach. Celebrating Christmas in our bathing suits was a first for us, and my family back home couldn't believe the pictures I sent them.

We spent most of our time in the hotel pool and on the beach doing handstands and soaking it all in. We cooked some meals in the room and tried different restaurants.

Seven days later, we reluctantly headed back north with beautiful memories and great tans. Instead of gas tanks in the trunk, this time we had sacks of oranges from the plantations, which I shared with my coworkers in Spuyten Duyvil.

My Czech friends were not quite as passionate about cars as I was. To them, cars were just transportation, and they were too shy to talk to dealers.

I read a lot about cars, so I happily went shopping with them, making ridiculous offers and driving the dealers crazy. They would say, "Oh that guy again,"—half funny and half serious.

I would say, "I always bring you money." We had to get the best deals we could, and we always used cash. I negotiated for a Cadillac, Buick, and Oldsmobile for the guys.

Spuyten Duyvil

Ladis in dune buggy

Chapter 20

Through a Czech friend I found my next job with Telaction Phone Corporation. I was interviewed for the position of telephone installer by the vice president of the company, who was a Cuban refugee himself.

There is a Czech saying: "Before anybody figures out that you don't know the job, you will learn it." I didn't dare try it two years earlier when Mercedes was looking for a mechanic. I would have loved to work on them, but I really didn't know that much about them yet, and I didn't want to risk ruining a customer's car. But this time I felt more confident, and my English was much better.

After two weeks of training, I was sent to the field to relocate telephones and install intercoms, amplifiers, and speakers in a shipping business warehouse. My company was also involved in closed-circuit televisions and cameras. I installed equipment in offices and small businesses. Some employees resented me putting in cameras; they thought their bosses were spying on them.

A few months later I was assigned to teach the job to two retired policemen and a youth. According to my boss, I had the most patience with new trainees. The cops did not do well with technical work and overall job ethics. Three weeks later I recommended their dismissal.

On the other hand, the youth was an excellent worker and a caring individual. He did good work. I appreciated him so much and ended up selling him my Buick with a hundred and twenty thousand miles on the odometer.

I felt bad two months later when the transmission blew up, and I even offered to partially pay for fixing it, which he refused. The company van that I was driving became my personal vehicle, until I bought a

Cadillac Sedan DeVille Brougham, which could carry almost as much in telephone equipment as the van had.

Through my job, I heard about a program sponsored by New York City that offered English lessons to immigrants. A group of elderly women from the Madison Avenue Presbyterian Church volunteered to teach on a one-to-one basis. I signed up for it and Gertrude was assigned as my teacher. She was born in Austria and had taught in the city school system. She taught me British English, with some explanations in German. I knew some German that my dad had taught me; the Russian that I was forced to learn for five years was not helpful at all.

I met with Gertrude once a week in the church for two hours. It was during one lesson that we heard voices from the gym, one floor above. She told me a group of other students were playing co-ed volleyball, which was one of my favorite sports. They were around my age, twenty-nine, and she took me to the gym to introduce me around. There were players from Greece, Peru, Czechoslovakia, and, of course, the United States. Some nights after my English lesson, I played with them, and we often went out for pizza and drinks afterward.

Chapter 21

I met many interesting people in this group and dated a few of the girls. But one caught my eye, because she was always yelling "easy" when I was serving. She wasn't much of a volleyball player, but she was enthusiastic and beautiful. Her name was Pat. When I worked in the city, sometimes I would meet her for lunch. She worked in an office in Times Square as an assistant buyer of children's clothes. One time, I told the receptionist outside her office that the phones had a problem, and I was there to fix them. Of course she didn't know anything about a phone problem, but I did get to see Pat and steal a kiss. On weekends we went to Bear Mountain to hike and explore, and many times we played tennis on Long Island.

We also went to church together to hear Reverend Norman Vincent Peale at Marble Collegiate, which was the first non-Catholic service I had attended since my youth. It was a whole new experience—without the rituals that I had known before. I felt encouraged and loved, and I enjoyed the atmosphere. For the first time in my life, I felt that God was real and could be approached directly, without a go-between.

Because of strong competition from New York Bell, my company, Telaction, went out of business. I had become familiar with the streets of New York City, so I took a job driving a cab. I really enjoyed driving for a living, and sometimes I gave Pat a ride in the cab. One time she needed to take her sewing machine to a special repair shop in downtown Manhattan, and it was too heavy for her to carry on the subway. Of course I didn't turn the meter on, so people were trying to flag me down and got pretty upset when I didn't stop for them.

I liked the challenge of getting customers to their destinations quickly. Some journeys were more fun than others, especially when they were late for work or in a hurry to catch a plane. They were hanging on to the straps in the back for dear life as I wove around traffic, through congestion, sometimes on sidewalks. Today I know there must have been angels with us back then, as I logged many miles without an incident.

But it could be a dangerous job too. One ride I picked up a passenger in Harlem, which is the upper part of Manhattan. As I started off to his destination, suddenly he said he had a gun and demanded my money. I felt something pushed against the seat into my back, and I believed him. Usually I would have had the Plexiglass partition between the front and back seat closed, but this time I didn't. So it was possible for him to grab me, or worse.

I said I had just started my shift and had only a bucket of change. He wanted that, and as I slowly picked it up and moved it up toward the partition, I quickly slammed the window shut with my elbow, spilling the bucket all over the seats. I held the air door lock down with my left hand so he couldn't jump out, laid on the horn, and drove as fast as I could safely, trying to attract the attention of a cop. None were in sight, so I pulled onto a side street, released the lock, and he jumped out. I had intended to run after him but lost sight of him. I was infuriated that he tried to rob me but thankful for my safety.

Another cab driver from our garage had seen me and reported me to the office for driving recklessly. I was reprimanded for not surrendering my money, which was the company policy. But I had worked hard for it, and I was not going to just hand it over. I vowed that I would never again drive a passenger to Harlem.

Bear Mountain, New York, 1974

Chapter 22

By this time, I had moved to a fifth-floor walk-up apartment in Brooklyn, which I shared with a fellow Czech cab driver named Karel. Since he liked to drive at night, and I preferred days, we contemplated purchasing our own cab and forming a Czech taxi company. It would have been possible if we were willing to pay $8000 for a required medallion and commit to staying in New York for several years. A medallion is a five-inch octagonal metal insignia attached to the hood of a cab. It is issued by New York State as proof of ownership and a license to operate a private cab company. But the idea didn't work out.

One night when Karel was working, I planned a special dinner of beef goulash and potatoes for my girlfriend, Pat. We had been having problems, and she had broken up with me a few days earlier. Having been together a year and a half, I realized I loved her and wanted to spend the rest of my life with her, so over candlelight I asked her to marry me. I didn't have a ring to give her, but she said yes anyway! I was so excited! And scared.

Even though it was November, there was a warm spell, and the next day we went to Jones Beach to celebrate our engagement with a bottle of champagne. We wore shorts and took lots of pictures.

We decided we wanted four children and picked out their names: Scott Jakob, we envisioned him as a professional football player; Marc Ladis, probably a doctor; Heidi Irena, maybe a novelist; and Holly Patricia, surely a famous designer.

In the afternoon the fog rolled in, adding to the magical moment. As the beach grass sparkled in the fading sunlight, it became too cold to stay. So we headed back to the car. But we had trouble finding it in the parking lot because the fog was so thick. That day is such a special memory for us.

We didn't want to tell anyone of our plans until we had talked to Pat's folks. Even though she had been living on her own for several years, I wanted to respect her and her parents and ask their permission. One weekend we drove to their place in Massachusetts, and I had a long talk with them. I asked for their permission to marry Pat and explained our plans to move out of New York City to Colorado. I also said that if they didn't permit me, I was going to kidnap her and take her with me anyway. They laughed and hugged me and were very happy for us.

Engagement Day, Jones Beach

Chapter 23

We wanted a May wedding in Pat's hometown of Acton, Massachusetts, and my future mother-in-law helped with our plans. She made arrangements with the local Baptist church that Pat grew up in. And she planned the reception and the cake.

Pat made a dress for her mother, her maid of honor, and her own wedding gown and veil. Suddenly, two weeks before our big day we had to change everything. The pastor had surgery, and we had to find another pastor and place for the reception. At the last minute, Mom tracked down Pat's youth minister from her high-school days and booked a lovely room for the reception.

Pat got to Acton a week before the wedding and made final arrangements—fitting dresses and picking up flowers and the cake. I drove up from New York later in the week, bringing Gertrude—my English teacher—with me. Pat's brother Bill and cousin Roger had a bachelor party for me on Friday night. We went out for drinks at a nearby pub, and Bill drove the big Lincoln Continental that we had borrowed for the wedding. Standing on chairs and singing, I told everyone in the bar I was getting married in the morning. Roger read me a list of "rights" I was giving up by getting married. There were many drinks and toasts to the groom. We finally left pretty late.

We were driving back to Acton on a back road when the night was suddenly filled with red and blue flashing lights. Two police cruisers pulled up behind us, and Bill slowly pulled over and stopped. An officer on a loud speaker ordered us to get out of the car slowly and raise our hands. We were afraid we all would be arrested for drinking, but that wasn't why we were pulled over.

We got out of the car with our hands up. The officers asked us what we had been doing for the last hour. Roger told the officer where we had been and added that we couldn't be arrested because I was getting married in the morning. The police officer explained that they were looking for three guys in a Continental who had just robbed a restaurant. But in the light of the spotlights, they could see we were not the ones they were looking for. An eyewitness to the crime said the robbers were all black men, and we were not. The officers congratulated me, wished me luck, and sent us on our way without even a ticket. What a relief! My wake-up call came awfully early the next morning, and what a story we three guys had to tell everyone!

Our wedding day was a gorgeous New England day with bright sunshine and warm temperatures. Pat and I got to the church early for pictures before the service. My stomach was in knots. Finally, everyone was seated and Roger, Bill, and I stood up front with Pastor Bill and watched as Pat came down the aisle with her father. He looked like he was about to cry; she looked beautiful. She finally was beside me and we held hands very tightly.

It was a small but beautiful ceremony. I especially liked having the American flag behind us on the stage where we took our vows. And it is in most of our pictures from that day. Naturally, my family couldn't come, so friends from Sokol—the name of the Czech volleyball team in New York—my roommate Karel, and a small group of family from Pat's side celebrated with us.

Pastor Bill said that marriage is a sacred vow before God and witnesses and that there will be challenges as well as good times. Any day of the week could be wonderful, but there will always come "those Thursdays" when you encounter problems. He encouraged us to trust God and our love and commitment to each other to get us through those times.

After the wedding, Bill drove the new Mr. and Mrs. Visner in the, by now, famous Continental across town to the reception hall. The car was decorated with "Just Married" signs, and cans were tied to the rear bumper. Bill honked the horn the whole way, leading a procession of cars behind us. By the time we got to the hall, the horn had died and was little more than a squawk.

We had a small cake and champagne at the reception. Mom had tried to find a punch tort, my favorite, but there was no such thing around there. A punch torte is a sponge cake made up of several colors and flavors of cake, soaked in rum, and covered in a glaze. I met Pat's cousins from out of state and several of her childhood girlfriends, who were married. I had promised the guys from the volleyball team that there would be single women there, and they were disappointed. But it was a fun party and everyone had a good time. We spent our wedding night at a nearby hotel. The next day we said our good-byes and headed back to New York.

We picked up Pat's things from her place in Manhattan. She also lived in a fifth-floor walk-up apartment, and the guys from the team helped carry it all down the stairs. I had only a few things to pack from my place in Brooklyn, including a bedroom set and silverware from a German lady who had lived in my building. She had given them to me when she moved back to Europe. A few days later we had packed it all in a van, hitched up a tow bar for my 1971 Plymouth Cricket with "Just Married" and "Colorado Is for Lovers" signs in the windows, and left the East Coast. Going west, people honked and smiled at us as they passed.

We had decided to move to Colorado because we thought it was the most beautiful state. The previous year we had driven cross country with a couple from Europe, stopping in many states, and we had stayed with friends there. The Rocky Mountains were spectacular, the air was dry, and the days were endless sunshine. And it was the West with real cowboys, like in my Rodokaps stories.

We had no job connections but lots of ambition and $700. We lived with friends for a couple of days until we found our own apartment in Arvada, a suburb of Denver. Two months later, we moved to a third-floor walk-up apartment in Lakewood, where we lived for five years. I worked as a welder and mechanic, and Pat did tailoring in a nearby cleaners.

Chapter 24

Back home, my mom became seriously ill, and I was worried that I might never see her alive again. Since I had been in the United States for five years, I was eligible to apply for citizenship and then I could get a passport. I planned to fly over and get a transit visa in Europe, good for a few days, to visit my family. Hopefully, as a US citizen, I would be allowed to enter Czechoslovakia and would be safe from arrest. I just didn't know; none of my friends had attempted to go back. I had to try.

Knowing that the naturalization process could take months, I attempted to speed it up by writing to the Office of President Gerald Ford, and I asked my local congressman for help. I never heard from the president, and promises from the senator's office never materialized.

Sadly, my mom passed away in the fall of 1976, just four months after we got married. Though I had considered this possibility when I planned my escape, it was still an awful loss for me. I am thankful that she was able to see our wedding pictures before that.

That winter, I passed a written and verbal test about American history and the Constitution. Then in a ceremony at city hall in Denver with other immigrants from all over the world, I took my oath and became a citizen of the United States of America! It was a beautiful day, and I was so proud to be part of the greatest nation in the world.

But it was a bittersweet victory, thinking about my mom and family. I immediately applied for a passport, knowing that it could take a few months. A visa was required to enter Czechoslovakia, but applying for that would have taken even longer. So we booked flights to Europe and hoped to get them over there. We would go a year later in the summer of 1977.

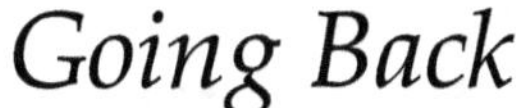

Going Back

Chapter 25

This trip was also to be our honeymoon since we had moved out west right after our wedding and started working right away. We landed in Frankfurt and stayed with a friend for a few days of sightseeing. I had met Jon at the camp in Italy, and he had immigrated to Germany, where he had a friend. He took us to the Czech embassy in Bonn, hoping to get a visa there, but it was closed. So another friend loaned us his Toyota 2000 GT and we set off to tour several countries, going first to Belgium.

We found the Czech embassy in Brussels, and with no problems we were granted transit visas for a three days' visit. We were so excited! We were among the first to be allowed back in to Communist Czechoslovakia after the 1968 invasion. We had a celebration dinner with chateaubriand at the Atomium restaurant that was located in the 1958 World's Fair park. It was at the top of a building shaped like an atom molecule and had a spectacular view of the city.

We drove back to Jon's and went on a shopping spree in Germany. Knowing that people in my country needed absolutely everything, we bought vegetables, fruit, liquor, cigarettes, shampoo, and soap. It was like Christmas in July. We loaded the Toyota and started at 5:30 in the morning from Ratingen, Germany. We got to the Czech border at 3:00 p.m. We were hungry and tired but anxious to see my family. We had no idea what to expect at the border and counted on our blue American passports to get us in safely.

There had been no traffic going in that direction. Of course few people were able, or desired, to go into the Communist country. We were asked stupid questions, and our passports and car papers were checked endlessly. As expected, they searched the car thoroughly—the trunk, the glove compartment, and door side pockets. They asked me to open the hood, and they took the engine air cleaner apart. They had special devices—mirrors on wheels—with which they checked under the car. They were looking for anything political, such as newspapers, cassettes, or books, but all they found were food items, cigarettes, and trinkets, which they did not confiscate.

Despite the frustration and anger, I had to be in control of my emotions and civilized if we had any chance of getting in. All this time, which seemed like an eternity, my wife quietly prayed for a safe, smooth passage.

Many calls were made to our town. Since there were only a handful of phones in the whole village, it took quite a while to locate someone who could verify my story that my father was not well.

After two and a half hours of interrogation and my assurance that the purpose of our stay was just a family visit, the head officer finally gave us back our passports. We were required to exchange $15 a day, per person, at a very unfavorable rate. Anything left unspent at the end of our visit would not be changed back to dollars. So we paid what was required and were finally allowed to enter. We were relieved and thrilled!

Chapter 26

I was overjoyed that it was possible for me to visit. Of course we didn't know that just two days earlier the Czech government had passed an amendment that made short transit visas possible. Looking back now, I see God's hand and His incredible timing.

So many emotions went through my head at once. We drove familiar roads through villages that were even more gray and dilapidated than I remembered six years earlier, but I eagerly anticipated seeing my family again. There were few street lights anywhere, so it was very dark and difficult to read signs. The only phones were in the post office, the police station, and local doctors. There was no way to inform my family of our arrival, so this was a complete surprise for them.

My dad's house was already dark, as he went to bed early, and waking him up was never so joyful! Pat knocked on his door, and it took him a few minutes to answer. It was difficult to see us clearly in the dim light, but eventually he recognized me. Through my tears, I could hear him saying over and over, "My boy is here, my boy is here!" We went into his room and sat with him for a while. There wasn't much talking, just deep looks and holding hands. How do you squeeze six years of sorrow and separation into two hours of joy?

I chuckled as I watched my wife and Dad holding hands and trying to communicate. He spoke German to her, and when she didn't understand, he repeated it louder. She still didn't comprehend. He was wondering why this beautiful woman didn't respond. My heart was overflowing with this pleasant confusion. We took Daddy with us to my brother's and sister's apartments a mile away. Again, tears of joy and endless questions about how, when, and how long?

In my brother's eyes, I saw a spark of admiration as if to say, "Look what my little brother did." Suddenly, years of joking and teasing about my plan to escape were exchanged for pride. My brother and his wife gave us their bedroom for the night. We were exhausted and a little fearful but happy to be there.

The next day we had to register with the local police. We had to inform them where we were going, whom we were seeing, and show them our papers. We also drove to the visa office in Pilsen to try to extend them. We wanted to visit my other sister in Moravia, which was a day's drive away.

Our visas were extended for two weeks, so we went to the US embassy in Prague to let them know we were in the country, in case we needed help. We gave them all our information about where we would be in Czechoslovakia and contacts back in America. While we were walking in Wenceslav Square, we were approached by a black market person who spoke English; he wanted to exchange money for triple the going rate. It was way too dangerous to consider; he could have been an agent in disguise. We declined.

We drove to Moravia and spent a few days with my family out there. They didn't have as many hardships as in Nyrsko and a few more material necessities.

When we returned to my brother's place in the western part of Czechoslovakia, we were greeted by my terrified family who told us about two visits by government agents while we had been gone. I had fully expected to be interrogated by the secret police during this visit, so I was not surprised. Any official could have created a scenario where I would have been detained and held on fabricated charges. Even as American citizens, we were in their jurisdiction, and the US State Department would have very little power to dispute alleged charges.

But I had great faith in my US passport. And I had instructed my brother on what to do if I got arrested and failed to return. He was to take Pat to the US embassy in Prague, where she would be safe. Thankfully we never had to use that plan!

Three agents showed up the next morning in their black limos. As polite as they were, there was a cautious undertone. They addressed me as "Mr. Visner" and politely waited every time I turned to my wife to translate the conversation. They were mostly interested in what information about Czech military installations I had given to FBI agents in the United States. They were convinced that escapees like me were asked about their locations. Of course this never happened. No agents were interested in me. No one had questioned me when I got to America, except a beggar looking for money.

After an hour of discussion and my insistence that I was never questioned by the FBI, I said there was nothing else to talk about, since they didn't believe my answers. They apologized and left, and my brother and his wife were greatly relieved. Obviously, my US citizenship had protected me and commanded their respect.

Agents like these, five years earlier, had come to my dad's house, as part of the intimidation of my family because of my escape. My clothes were taken, even though they had little value to anyone and were probably dumped somewhere later. But the trauma and the shame my family felt was long lasting and heartbreaking. I was so sorry they had to endure that humiliation.

My dad's house had only a cold water faucet and a dry toilet in a closet. It was heated with a little wood-burning stove, which was also used for cooking. Newer buildings like my brother's had a flush toilet in one room, a sink and tub with hot and cold water in another room, and a kitchen with both. The plant behind his neighborhood provided the hot water and heat for the area. At one point during our visit, the workers at this plant went on vacation, leaving many people with no hot water for a week. We took sink baths with water heated on the gas stove.

There were long lines for everything. People waited hours for things they needed. Sometimes they waited for a special item that wasn't widely available. One time, people stood in line overnight for hand-painted, porcelain, three-piece coffee sets that were expected to arrive at the store. Usually this beautiful Czech handcraft would have been exported and wouldn't have been available to the public. We had a contact person and a 100 krona tip ($5 today) under the table, which helped us secure one of the sets.

During our visit, we went to a friendly butcher in the next town after regular business hours. A small bribe of $5 resulted in two full bags of meats, and I can still see my brother shaking his head in disbelief over the amount we were able to buy. Normally we would not have been allowed to buy that much. Quantities were rationed according to the number of people in your family. Of course, a deal like that could have resulted in imprisonment for the butcher, if the authorities had found out.

To my brother's astonishment, we also bought a case of bottled Coca Cola—quite a treat at that time—and a case of beer. We gave a small boy $1 to carry the boxes to our car; he was thrilled!

Free enterprise was, of course, dead. All companies and businesses were owned and run by the government, with methods that stunted any growth or prosperity. Pat commented that my homeland seemed to be stuck in a time warp in the 1960s, isolated from progress that Western countries enjoyed. Girls in Czechoslovakia still wore beehive hairdos and miniskirts like in the 60s, and the Beatles and Elvis could only be heard over Voice of America.

Pat was in culture shock. The food was greasy, the air was full of smoke from plants and cigarettes, and the only safe drink was bottled water. Czech coffee, called Turkish coffee, was made by putting coffee grounds in a cup to which hot water was added. Then sugar and cream were stirred in, and you had to wait for the "mud" to settle to the bottom, since it didn't dissolve, before you could drink it. If you weren't careful, you could get a mouthful of chewy grounds stuck in your teeth.

There weren't many vegetables, just sauerkraut and cucumbers, but lots of potatoes and dumplings with heavy sauces. We felt sluggish and bloated.

Conditions were so appalling we would have loved to bring my entire family to America, but that was legally impossible. Before leaving the country, we shopped at Tuzex and bought the family clothes and other necessities to make their lives a little more bearable.

Chapter 27

After two weeks, we left Czechoslovakia and drove toward Austria. We were both glad to leave but sad to say good-bye to my family. As hard as it was to be allowed into Czechoslovakia, it was much easier for us to leave. We showed our US passports and officers searched the car and gave us very little trouble.

What a contrast a few kilometers made. There were the same beautiful rolling hills and forests in both countries, but private ownership on the Austrian side meant the homes and businesses were well taken care of. Buildings were patched, painted, and decorated with numerous flower boxes. Fields and even forests looked well manicured.

In comparison, the Czech side was very neglected. Buildings were falling apart and overgrown. We breathed a sigh of relief not only because we were safe in western Europe again, but also because the air itself was brighter and cleaner. It wasn't polluted by factories, cars, and coal-burning homes.

Since this journey was also our honeymoon, we stayed six more weeks, traveling through the capitals of Europe. Our first stop was in Vienna, Austria, where we ate at a restaurant called "Budapest." We drove to Schonbrunn and were awed by the beautiful landscape and palace of Maria Teresa.

We toured an armory museum then drove to Mautendorf, where we met up with Gertrude, my English teacher from New York City. She spent her summers in her home country. It was a charming village, and the Hotel Steffner Wallner was full of amazing antiques. The car had brake problems, and Pat had stomach problems, but both were solved in a day. We visited a castle in Tamsweg and met a gal from Pennsylvania working in a linen shop.

The next day we drove to Venice, Italy. It was saturated with American tourists, and there was lots of souvenirs for sale. We had a great dinner but didn't sleep well because we were awakened really early by a delivery barge outside our hotel window. We took a gondola ride, of course, and really saw up close how badly the buildings were falling apart.

From Venice we drove to Florence and enjoyed a craft market. Then on to Rome for a few days. We saw the Colosseum, threw coins in the Trevi fountain, and spent an entire day at the Vatican. The furniture, sculptures, and tapestries were breathtaking! The Sistine Chapel with its huge painted ceiling by Michelangelo and the enormous altar at St. Peter's Cathedral were the highlights of our visit there. Our best meal in Rome was at a Chinese restaurant.

We left Rome and headed toward Monaco. We drove through thirty tunnels and saw lots of places to have a drink, but no bathroom facilities. That night we slept in the car and arrived in the tiny principality the next day. We watched the changing of the guard at the palace, ate crepes, and stared at people entering the casino in the middle of the town. The hotel we stayed in was nice, even though Pat's hairdryer blew a fuse in the room and the bed broke.

From Monaco we went to Marseille, France, for a night. It had a smelly fish market, but we had a good meal at the restaurant "San Francisco."

The next day we drove to Barcelona, Spain. It was hot and humid in mid-August, and most of Europe was on vacation. We walked miles through a cactus garden and craft show. The next day we got to Rosas by Costa Brava and enjoyed a few days of sightseeing, dining on good food, and watching fireworks off the beach.

Our next stop was Montchanin, France. We drove through hail the size of rocks and finally stopped at a Novotel, one of a chain of hotels in Europe. The next day was spent with cousins of mine. We had the best pizza and lasagna with them and talked till late at night. My cousin had married an Italian and their children were learning English, so we spoke Czech, French, Italian, and English!

The next day, on to Paris! We explored the city for two days. We enjoyed a show at the Moulin Rouge and saw Pigalle, Sacre Coeur, and

Montmatre, where a chalk artist had drawn a huge picture of Christ's face on the sidewalk. His eyes seemed to follow us.

We saw Notre Dame Cathedral, Le Louvre—including the Mona Lisa—walked the Champs Elysee, and climbed the Eiffel Tower. We drove to Versailles and had a great meal in a Japanese restaurant.

Paris was a wonderful finish to our first trip together around Europe. Pat was in love with it all. She really enjoyed the castles and hearing the languages. She made use of her high-school French in France and Belgium and was inspired to learn more languages. She was hooked and couldn't wait to return.

We drove back to Jon's in Germany and a few days later flew back to the United States. It had been an exhausting but satisfying journey, and I was encouraged to know that we could go into my country and see my family again.

Chalk artist in Paris

Chapter 28

Back home in Colorado we got back to reality. I responded to an ad for a "shakeman" at a construction site, despite not having a clue exactly what it was.

I got to the job site early where new homes were being built and learned that wood shakes were a roofing material. I figured out the proper application technique and talked my way into the job.

Six months later, I started my own roofing company and secured a contract with Scufka Shelton, a local builder who kept me busy for several years. They were building many homes at the time, and I just roofed one after another.

Meanwhile, we had found a piece of property, much bigger than we needed for a single family home, but it was such a great deal. It was almost fourteen acres of land. It was on a hill with a fantastic view of the mountain range, pine trees across the street, and lots of open land all around. I made many important contacts with other contractors on my job and bartered work with them when building our first house in Parker, Colorado.

The old country habit of paying with cash resulted in us having no credit and not being able to secure a building loan. So we built it from our paychecks, even though friends called it insane.

Weekends were spent gathering and sorting discarded two-by-four studs, nails, plywood, and other building materials that I brought home from work. I built an outhouse on the property for use during construction. It had a heart on the door and comics served as wallpaper inside.

Through bartering, we were able to finish the exterior of the house, and, two years later, I secured a small loan to complete the inside. Finally, after three long years and much hard work it was done. It had certainly tested our young marriage; it seemed we were looking at studs and no walls for a very long time.

Finally, we left the one-bedroom apartment that we had been in for five years and moved into our beautiful four-bedroom, twenty-seven-hundred-square-foot house on fourteen acres overlooking the Rocky Mountains. I was actually living my childhood dream that I had read about in Rodokaps, owning a piece of America in the West!

We built a big house expecting our four children—that we had dreamed of—to fill it. Maybe now that we were in the house, they would come along.

Site of our first house in Colorado

In Sickness and Health

Chapter 29

Six months after we moved into our new home, Pat became seriously ill. She was pale, out of breath all the time, and had no energy. She thought it was just anemia. She developed big bruises on her arms and legs, though she had not hit anything. She passed out when a friend was giving her a haircut and was taken to the hospital. By the time I got there, she was conscious but could not talk. Aphasia, the doctors told me. She was also jaundiced.

She was given several pints of blood, and they started running many tests to figure out what was wrong with her. I was asked hundreds of questions: where had we been, what had we eaten, what had we done that was unusual?

I was petrified. I called my in-laws when I got home and told them Pat was sick. That first week, I drove to the hospital in Denver after work each day. She recovered her ability to speak very soon, but she was still yellow and had a moon face from the steroids she was receiving. She was in good spirits despite the frequent blood drawing.

Lab work showed her blood platelets were extremely low. Her body was destroying her own blood cells, an autoimmune response requiring more transfusions. Since the doctors did not yet know what it was, they gave her steroids and antibiotics. There were more questions, and more doctors became involved. They hinted it could be something serious, but they did not give it a name. A week later they decided it was a rare disease called thrombotic thrombocytopenic purpura (TTP). If she had had kidney or liver failure, they would have been sure. But she also would have been dead.

It was a potentially fatal disease. Medical books at the time said there was an 80 percent mortality rate. But when she asked what her chances were, the doctor said, "50/50."

She replied, "Oh, that is good." She was not scared at all!

Pat's mom was in the medical profession, and when I told her the doctor's diagnosis, they flew out to Denver the next day from Massachusetts, sure they were going to bury their second daughter. I was real glad to see them, and they stayed at our house for several weeks.

One night there was a possibility that Pat's spleen was going to have to be removed, but things calmed down and she came through that. Since it was such a rare disease, with unspecified treatments, doctors were not sure how to treat it. So they gave her chemotherapy several times and an experimental treatment called plasmapheresis. A representative from *Forbes* magazine was on hand to watch the first procedure because it was so new.

She was hooked up to a machine. One tube took blood out of her femoral artery in her thigh. The blood went through a separation process where damaged platelets were discarded and fresh platelets, which had been donated, were added to the remaining blood parts before being returned through a tube in an arm. If more blood was taken out than what was being put back in, she would faint.

If her platelet count failed to stay up in a "normal" range, she had to go through this treatment again. During her two weeks in the hospital and a few weeks after she got home, she had this done four times. Plasmapheresis has since become the prescribed treatment for several diseases in addition to TTP. Pat kept her Bible with her at all times, during treatments, and in her room, and it seemed to give her strength.

People from the church that we attended brought me meals, visited Pat in the hospital, and prayed for her recovery. After two long weeks, she finally came home, weak but alive.

Her parents stayed with us another week, caring for Pat and me. They really helped out a lot, doing laundry, cleaning, and comforting. Her sister lived forty-five minutes away in Colorado Springs, but the two were not very close at that time. Pat's sister cooked and brought up an entire Thanksgiving dinner! Turkey with all the trimmings. What a lot of work and a wonderful expression of her love. We were so touched by that, and what a celebration we had! We had so much to be thankful for.

After chemotherapy, plasmapheresis, steroids, and other meds, she was declared, "in remission." Her primary doctor, one of thirteen working to heal her, admitted it must have been God's will for her to survive. He had no other explanation for it. He told us there had been another case of TTP and that patient had received all the treatments that Pat had, and she had died. What a miracle!

At that time, in the early 1980s, there was no testing for AIDS or HIV yet. Although Pat received many units of blood and platelets, none of them were tainted with hepatitis or any disease. Another blessing!

Chapter 30

I too had several brushes with death. When I was twelve years old in Czechoslovakia, I was picking wild blueberries with friends on a hillside above the outdoor theater in Nyrsko. Somehow I lost my footing and fell six meters (eighteen feet), landing on my back on the stone steps below that were part of the outdoor theater sets.

I lay there awhile, until I regained consciousness, with my friends just staring at me wondering if I was dead. Nothing was broken, so I limped home and did not tell my mother. Had she known I was climbing that hill by the theater, she would have scolded me. I had already promised to go blueberry picking with her later that day, and when she asked why I was moving funny I just said I was sore from playing soccer.

When I was twenty-two, I was riding my Norton motorcycle back to Nyrsko from my job in the coal mines. I was about two-thirds of the way there when something flew into my helmet and repeatedly stung me. I felt dizzy so I pulled over and collapsed under a tree. There was no one to help me. I was on a back road that very few people used. I do not know for how long I was out cold; it could have been just a few minutes or hours. It was summer so the sun set late. I finally got back on the road and had no further problems with bee stings until twenty-six years later in Colorado.

I was walking on our little patch of grass in front of our second house, when I felt a sting in my big toe. I did not see any bump or sting mark, but later on I felt dizzy, I couldn't breathe, and I slid down to the garage floor as Pat called the ambulance. She was hysterical with fear.

By the time they arrived, I was unconscious, my blood pressure was very low, and the paramedic had a hard time finding a vein to put in an IV. They had to put a tube down my throat so I could breathe. I was in anaphylactic shock. Instead of a normal reaction, like a red bump, my whole body overreacted and was about to shut down my organs, one by one, in order to "save" me, but thus killing me.

The paramedics said I would not make it to the hospital alive, by ambulance, so they called in a helicopter, and it landed right in front of our house. Too bad I could not enjoy the ride. I did not regain consciousness until later on in the emergency room.

After much testing, doctors said I was allergic to several kinds of bees and another sting could kill me. It was very hard to admit that such a tiny creature had that much power over my life, but I had to accept it. I was to carry an epinephrine injector pen with me at all times. In case of another reaction, it would keep my heart going until I got to a hospital. To this day, I have one with me at all times.

One winter we had a severe blizzard in Parker. Powerful winds howled and blew the snow sideways. There was no visibility—a complete whiteout—and it was really cold. It was Christmastime and we were expecting several feet of snow. A neighbor called to say someone was stuck in a car in a snowdrift on a nearby road. According to him, our house was closest to his location and he asked me to go look for him.

Without hesitation, I pulled on my heavy snow boots, jacket, hat, gloves, and took a snow shovel with me. I stepped into knee-deep snow and made my way down the long driveway to our gate. The snow had drifted so high all I saw were the two posts on either side of it. Through the howling wind and snow, I walked a total of several hundred meters (about a thousand feet) in both directions on the unplowed road trying to find and rescue whoever was supposedly stranded. The snow was so deep I made very slow progress, holding the shovel in front of my face to protect it from the biting wind and snow. I was so sure I would find this person that I kept going, not even considering my own safety and unsure if I was still on the road or if I had wandered off it. I was hopelessly lost.

While walking I fell down, and it felt so comfortable and warm, away from the wind, I just wanted to stay down and rest and regain strength. Suddenly, I woke up scared, not knowing how long I had been asleep, and realized that being so tired I could have frozen to death. At this point, no longer thinking about rescuing anyone but myself, I just tried desperately to find my way back to the house. Till today I don't know how I made it back up that long hill without Divine help.

Finally, I could see the silhouette of our house and heard heavenly bells coming from it. Pat was standing in the doorway shaking a set of Austrian cow bells, trying to direct me to the door. I had been gone over two hours, and she was frantic with worry. As it turned out, the person who was lost was several miles down the road from us and was found safe. God certainly was present and protecting us in these and other times.

Chapter 31

Having babies is a normal part of most marriages, but it is truly a miracle from God. Months and years ticked by in our marriage with no offspring. The doctors said we were both healthy and couldn't find an explanation. As we watched others have babies, we questioned our motives to see if we wanted children for the wrong reasons; we questioned our qualifications, sure that we could provide a loving home; we questioned why other people who didn't want children had them and not us. We wondered if we had a sin too big for God to forgive and if this was our punishment.

There were many questions and emotions involved: anger, frustration, jealousy, sadness, resentment, acceptance. Why? Why not? Pat and I were in a support group and learned that we were in a cycle of mourning for our lost dream of Scott, Marc, Heidi, and Holly. One week I would be jealous of another family, and the next week I would accept the situation and not be too angry. Pat's emotions ran in cycles of hope, anger, depression, jealousy, but rarely accepting. It was a constant roller coaster and it was stressful.

Meeting new people at church was hard; they all had children and just assumed everyone else did too. The first question usually was, "How many children do you have?" We felt like outcasts and abnormal. Sometimes I wanted to scream, "Not everyone has children! We are not childless by choice!" We tried to avoid Mother's Day and Father's Day events. Well-meaning friends didn't understand and used clichés like, "Oh just relax," "It will happen," or "Take a vacation."

We tried treatments that had helped others and even considered adoption. But we were told we were too old. At that point, Pat was only thirty-five, certainly not too old to have a baby! We knew that God was in control of all aspects of our lives. The Bible tells how He made a teenage virgin, Mary, pregnant with Jesus; her cousin Elizabeth, a barren and old woman gave birth to John the Baptist; Sarah was ninety years old when she gave birth to Isaac; and after years of being barren Rachel had two sons.

It is a couple's problem, not the wife's or husband's. Infertility can be very stressful in a marriage and many couples break up because of it, thinking they will be able to have children with a different spouse. We spent years agonizing over it, talking, praying, bargaining, confessing, and whatever we could think of. Both of us came to the same conclusion: we wanted each other with or without children. If that meant no kids, then so be it, we would accept that. Together we could handle it.

Finally, after more than ten years, we had to accept that it wasn't going to happen. We realized God could have given us children, but He had a different plan for us. We didn't know the reasons why, we just had to trust Him. If we had had four children in Colorado, we probably would not have gone to Czechoslovakia as often or moved around this country so much. This way, we have been able to help so many people and have been blessed with so much. We have enjoyed living in New England, in the West, and now in the southeast United States. And God has brought many "sons" and "daughters" into our lives over the years to nurture and help fill that emptiness.

Transportation

Chapter 32

Cars are my passion, and I have been able to own quite a number of them. In Czechoslovakia, people worked a very long time to afford a car. Some people never got one or a license to drive. My car there was a Fiat 600.

In America, the possibilities are endless. To date, I have cared for thirty-six vehicles. I had a 1967 Ford Mustang convertible in New York City, but I had to sell it after my eight-track player was stolen and my roof was sliced a couple of times. Too bad I could not have kept it!

I traded that for my first Cadillac. In Colorado, I owned a 1967 Peugeot that blew a head gasket one day; huge clouds of smoke filled the neighborhood. Neighbors were not too thrilled about that!

I had pickup trucks to carry tools and supplies for my construction business, and Pat drove a bright orange Fiat all over Colorado for her job.

My 1974 Chevy Blazer took us to Massachusetts for Christmas one year. We had padded and insulated the walls, hung curtains, and slept in it along the way, but the windshield cracked because of the severe cold.

My 1982 Chevy Silverado was haunted; the wipers would surprise me and swipe the windshield anytime they wanted. My small Fiat hauled a refrigerator to a house, and my Toyota GT coughed its way up Pikes Peak in Colorado Springs.

At one point in our first house, I had four vehicles in the driveway. I had built my garage extra long, which included a grease pit. During one blizzard, I had three cars in it; one was parked sideways in the front.

I tried to make excellent deals buying and selling cars, even completing one sale by flashlight when there was a power failure at the dealership.

Our black Labrador puppy was also part of a deal. He was supposed to be a guard dog but was really friendly to strangers and posed no threat at all. When a buyer came to look at the truck I was selling, Duke was all over him. I said I would throw in the dog and his insulated dog house that I had built, if he bought the truck. He took the truck, Duke, and his house, and everyone was happy!

Most of my cars have been manual transmissions. Pat loves to drive a stick also; she learned to drive on her mother's VW Bug. I have upgraded over the years to newer vehicles requiring fewer repairs and will eventually need only one car between us. But not yet!

Chapter 33

We have been able to visit Europe almost every year. For several trips we flew to Munich or Nuremberg, Germany, and took a train into Czechoslovakia. Rental car agreements in Germany did not allow us to take cars into Communist countries including Czechoslovakia, because often they would be stolen. So our friend Martin oftentimes loaned us his car.

Once, we borrowed his Mercedes with pneumatic suspension, which was fed by a compressor under the hood. The rubber drums were filled with air and could adjust the rear suspension of the car. It was very luxurious, and the height of the vehicle could be lowered or raised while driving. A stone punctured one of the drums and, despite efforts to fix it with my brother and brother-in-law, it leaked air and the rear end of the car hung very low to the ground. We looked like we were carrying something very heavy in the trunk. As we prepared to leave the country, we emptied the trunk of everything, moved our suitcases to right behind the front seats, and shifted them all the way forward.

When we got to the first gate at the border crossing, of course we looked very suspicious. The five guards, about twenty years old with machine guns, checked our passports and thoroughly searched the empty trunk—they were so sure they would find contraband or a person hiding, trying to escape from the country. We laughed to ourselves at their frantic determination to find anything illegal. If they had found something, they would have been assured of a promotion.

I gave a long explanation about the air suspension, which they had never heard of before. All this time there was a constant "hiss" as the air continued to leak. Reluctantly, realizing their own ignorance, we were allowed to proceed to the second gate and main customs building where our passports were checked again against Interpol data. More questions came our way: where had we been, what had we done, whom did we talk to? Our passports were held while they did a search with mirrors rolled under the car. And, once again, they searched the empty trunk!

Two hours later, we were permitted to pass through the massive gate made up of a steel beam imbedded in concrete structures. The third gate was in Germany. The guards had observed the whole situation and were mostly laughing about it.

One year, Martin asked us to drive his Renault Le Car into Czechoslovakia to give to his wife and sons for Christmas. By United States standards it was a small unimpressive car, but by Czech standards it was impressive. We drove it into the country from outside of Munich where Martin was living. It was full of presents for the family, and we put a big red bow on top of it.

Martin had escaped after 1978 and eventually he was able to obtain freedom for his wife and sons by repaying the Czech government for their "education." In reality, it was a penalty for their leaving.

Changes

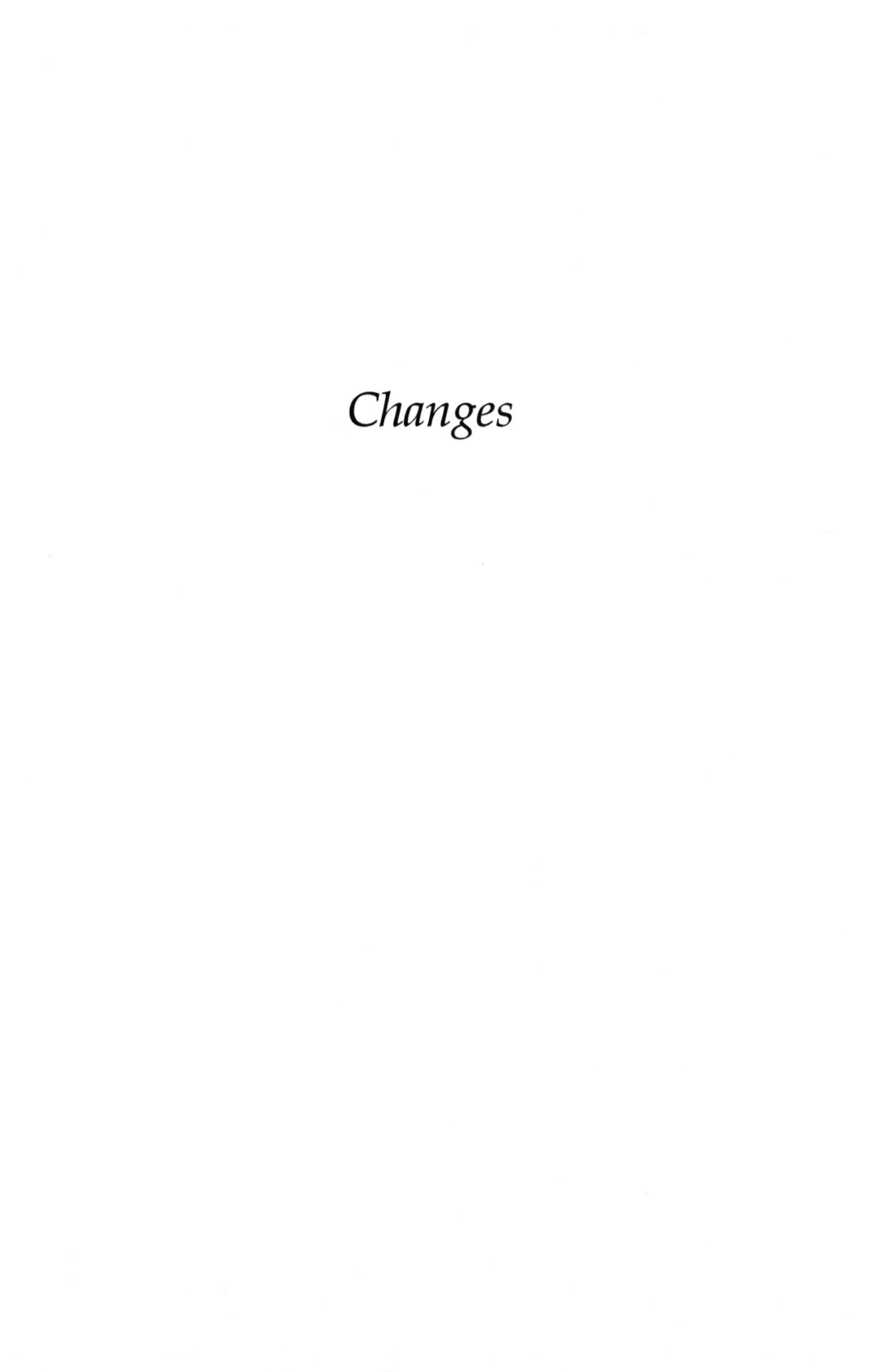

Chapter 34

Pat had grown up going to a Baptist church in Massachusetts, so faith in God was an easy choice for her. She believed He was real and involved in every aspect of our lives.

My church in Czechoslovakia had no meaning for me, and atheism was encouraged under Communism. You were mocked if you expressed a belief in God rather than the party. I learned to rely only on myself, and I thought I was in control of my life.

One day in Colorado, a fellow carpenter invited me to a Bible study, and I started reading the Word of God. I learned He knows all about me and loves me just as I am; that Jesus was sinless, yet He died for my sins. I had never known a love like this and wanted to know more about this Creator of the universe.

Our new pastor named Josh was an ex-Mississippi State linebacker. I admired him for his humility and dedication to the Lord, but what I liked the most was that he was such a formidable man who certainly didn't have to be afraid of anyone, yet he was so humble and had a strong faith in God.

He taught me many things, but the most important lesson was that nothing in my life happened by chance. God had a plan for me and was guiding me step by step. The encounters with the US soldiers in 1945 in my home, the Rodokaps stories, and Voice of America broadcasts, I could see how all these events fell into place so precisely, because it was God's master plan and destiny for me.

It has been a process over the years, growing in my faith as I trust Him more. I believe part of God's plan for us was downsizing and building our second home in a beautiful part of Parker, Colorado, called the Pinery. Rather than borrowing for a mortgage, as our friends and family suggested, we prayed about it and decided to follow the biblical principle that says, "Let no debt remain outstanding"(Romans 13:8). We built the house from the profit we made on the sale of the first house. It proved to be the right decision for us, as I injured my back right after we moved in. I was out of work for six months, and if we had owed a lot of money we would have struggled to pay the bills.

That house also had a view of Denver and the Rockies. It was passive solar with a solarium in the front. I built very wide walls on the north side, and Pat made insulation curtains for all the windows. We heated it with a wood-burning stove.

Having no mortgage also freed us up to make yearly mission trips to Czechoslovakia. We organized a clothing drive through our church, Church of the Rock in Castle Rock, Colorado. Our basement was full of clothes that we shipped by Lufthansa Cargo Freight, directly to the underground church in my hometown.

Normally, people were required to pay a duty on any gifts received from overseas. The government used that as a deterrent to discourage families in the West from sending things. But because they were used clothes, the church didn't have to pay customs. That was a special blessing that we had not anticipated.

The pastor of the little church in Nyrsko took some clothes to a small village in Russia to share with them, because the people there had next to nothing. They considered the Czechs the capitalists. Even in early April some of the kids in the village were barefooted. We heard there were fights over the jeans, by far the most popular item.

Chapter 35

In 1988, we smuggled Czech Bibles into the country. We were inspired after reading, *God's Smuggler* by Brother Andrew, a Dutch missionary. We bought ten Bibles with bright red covers, from the International Bible Society in Colorado Springs. We knew the car would be thoroughly searched, so hiding them would have been pointless. Before we got to the border, we prayed the smuggler's prayer: "Lord, when You were on this earth, You made blind eyes see. We ask now, Lord, that You make seeing eyes blind." We left the Bibles on the back seat of the car, covered only with a thick *Chicago Tribune* newspaper. Our church in Colorado knew when we would be at the border and were praying for us.

The guards were going to confiscate the newspaper because no foreign political publications were allowed in the country. In an attempt to keep the Bibles covered, I asked the guards if I could keep just the sports section for my brother. There was an article about the Chicago Blackhawks, his favorite team.

They agreed and I carefully separated the newspaper, keeping the red books covered. They never saw the ten Bibles hidden in plain sight! God certainly must have blinded them! We rejoiced as we drove through the crossing, thankful for His protection. At the time, we had no idea how much danger we had been in. If we had been discovered, we could have been forbidden from entering the country ever again, or I could have been jailed, never to see Pat or my family again. But God answered all our prayers and we and the Bibles arrived safely.

We didn't quite know to whom we might give the Bibles—we thought maybe the local priest, family, or friends. As we prayed about them, eventually God revealed His choices. We went to a Mass in the local Catholic Church. Including my brother and sister and us, there were ten people at the service. I struggled to translate the sermon for my wife, but the message was so impersonal and unclear, even I had a hard time trying to make sense of it. It was nothing compared to what we were used to in our church back in Colorado.

On top of that, in the unheated church it was about 7°C (40°F), and our hands and feet were freezing. There was a steady stream of steam coming off the priest's bald head, and it definitely wasn't because of a fiery message! He hurried out of the church without talking to anyone, and we agreed that he was not going to get a Bible from us. God had much grander plans.

The first one to receive a Bible was the elderly mother of a friend of ours, who was bedridden. She had commented that she had always wanted one of her own, and we gladly filled her wish. Other Bibles were distributed to family and close friends, as we were led.

But the last one to be given away was the most exciting. One late night while visiting my sister, there was a knock on the door. The wide-eyed couple introduced themselves as the pastors of the local underground church. They had heard about us and the Bibles and wanted to invite us to visit their congregation. We knew they would appreciate having the last one.

We visited their church and shared the gospel and sang the same songs in two languages. Friends who came with us couldn't understand how we knew them, but He is the same God wherever we go. That was so fantastic! It was to this pastor that we sent the shipments of clothing.

They also introduced us to a needy family in Moravia who was looking for a child's wheelchair. They had adopted a girl with no legs, and the only wheelchairs in the country were adult sized. There was a long waiting list for them, and someone had to die for one to become available.

They asked us if we could find one for her and send it from America. She was a beautiful six-year-old girl, full of energy and quite agile, scooting along on her hands. She played the piano and sang while her mother played the guitar.

When we got back home, it was easy for me to find a child's wheelchair in a hospital supply store in Denver. We outfitted it with pockets, pillows, and seat belts to prevent her little body from falling out. I built a sturdy crate and Lufthansa Cargo shipped it to them.

On our next trip to Moravia, we took my sister and her husband with us to visit this precious family. We found our shipping crate converted into a jungle gym, and Katka and her sisters climbing and swinging from it. The wheelchair was a perfect fit. It gave her greater mobility, and she was zipping around the rooms in it. We were so blessed by this family, which included two biological children and three handicapped ones.

Later on, we learned from my sister that Katka's story was featured in a national ladies' magazine. It was mostly factual, except when it came to who donated the wheelchair. Communist propaganda credited a pair of Swedish doctors with providing it for her, instead of stating that an American couple had supplied it. We were mad but not surprised at the government, because I knew how the system operated. It was part of the Communist policy to denounce anything that was decent and honorable, especially if it came from the West.

Despite the lie, we were satisfied that we had fulfilled a special need for her, no matter who got the credit. Today, Katka is a talented vocalist who sings for the Lord.

Chapter 36

Every year God added more people to our circle of friends that we visited in Czechoslovakia: distant cousins, classmates, neighbors. We have bought tires, food for people and animals, and just spent time with them over a beer or coffee.

Many young people in the Czech Republic have touched our lives. Some were for just a short time, others for a lifetime. One year, we met a charming girl who had a growth deficiency problem. She was always going to be the size of a child. We sent her clothes and shoes; it was very hard to find ones that didn't look like a child's. She has since gotten married and has a daughter of her own.

Another time, at a country western bar, we met a teenager named Eva. We were demonstrating line dancing and encouraging people to join us on the dance floor. She was the only one brave enough to try, and she spoke excellent English. Pat offered to connect her with students in the United States to be pen pals, but Eva wanted to write to Pat instead. They wrote for several years, and we saw her a few times when we went to Czechoslovakia.

Another friend, Mia, had not been able to have children with her husband, Stefan. He had a disease called Marfan Syndrome, an inherited disorder that affects the heart, eyes, and skeleton. It can cause dislocation of the ocular lens, skeletal abnormalities, and heart problems, which can be life threatening. He had an affair and fathered a child who also had the disease. Stefan died and, despite his infidelity, Mia was willing to help care for his daughter. Instead of being angry and jealous, she was forgiving and gracious, and seeking the best care for the girl. Mia asked if we could schedule a visit with an ophthalmologist. We did make arrangements for transportation to Slovakia and the doctor's appointment, but the girl's birth mother changed her mind at the last minute.

We met another woman in 1996. Jenn was from the United Kingdom and was married to a Czech. Both were zoologists and their house was a menagerie of reptiles and farm animals. She and Pat became fast friends, partly because they both spoke English and were free spirits. On every visit, we delegated time to take her to Germany for a fun day of breakfast, shoe shopping, sightseeing, and enjoying each other. Through the years, we have shared many laughs with her over cappuccinos and family parties.

Pat met a special young lady from the Czech Republic in a fabric store on Cape Cod, Massachusetts. We had moved there after sixteen years in Colorado and five years in Jupiter, Florida. Betka had been in America just a few years and was married to a musician from England. She came from Ostrava where I had worked in the coal mines. Pat and she liked the same things—castles, clothing design, exercise, healthy eating—and they became very close. Pat said that if she could design an ideal daughter, this is who she would be. Even when Betka returned to live in her country, and we moved around this country, we kept in touch, seeing her whenever we could, either in America or in Europe.

Other special people have come into our lives. Some were relatives, others were neighbors or friends. We have tried to encourage them and give them hope. "Oh that you would bless me and enlarge my territory!" (1 Chronicles 4:10). God certainly has enlarged our "territory" each time.

The Velvet Revolution happened in 1989. The wall came down, Communists were voted out of power, and the Russians left Czechoslovakia. My dad had always believed this system was not sustainable; unfortunately, he didn't live to see it collapse.

Borders were opened and people were free to travel. In 1991, Slovakia wanted to be their own sovereign country and separated from the Czech part. This was called the Velvet Divorce. It was a peaceful separation with no bloodshed. So Bohemia in the west and Moravia in the east made up the new Czech Republic.

We visited every year and saw changes each time. With no restrictions at the borders, there was less checking and sometimes we just waved our US passports while driving through; other times, the police stamped them. Now, in 2016, the crossings are not manned at all.

There are signs to tell you that you have entered the Czech Republic. Poor road conditions and some dilapidated buildings are still evidence of the old era, but foreign exchange offices and souvenir markets now line the roads.

Slowly, Czechs are again taking pride in their towns and improving things, fixing and painting buildings, and decorating with flower boxes. Many are opening their own businesses. In Nyrsko, two sisters have opened a coffee shop, there is a new bakery and children's clothing shop, a privately owned hair salon, and others. The European Union has poured euros into the country, building roads and sidewalks.

Monument in northern
Bohemia, to US liberators

My brother and niece by plaque on Nyrsko town hall, commemorating liberation by General Patton's Third Army

Chapter 37

After sixteen years in Colorado, we were tired of snow and wanted to live in the tropics. We had friends in Florida, so we visited them and bought a beautiful house in Jupiter. I worked in construction and Pat did alterations, both of us self-employed, so we had the flexibility to travel.

We decided having our own car in the Czech Republic was easier than borrowing or renting every time, so in 1996 we bought a 1991 Nissan Stanza and shipped it overseas from Jacksonville, Florida to Amsterdam. Two months later, we flew to the Netherlands to pick it up and drive to Czechoslovakia. We planned to store it in my brother's garage.

The agency that was transporting it suggested we not use the correct license plate for shipping because they were usually stolen by the crew for souvenirs, and a Florida one was really special. Since old license plates were not returnable, in Florida I attached an old one to the Stanza and carried the correct one in my suitcase.

At the Amsterdam harbor, the weather was horrible. We didn't bother changing the plate before we got to the Czech Republic, about a six hundred-kilometer drive (373 miles).

Arriving at the Czech border crossing, the biggest problem the guards had was where the front plate was; they were so sure it had been stolen. In Europe, cars are required to have both plates, in the front and back. We explained that Florida required only one plate. They never checked our paperwork, which had the correct license plate number on it, and we did not want to confuse them anymore.

They let us pass and when we got to my brother's garage, we put the right one on the car, and the old one was added to his collection of plates that I had brought him over the years. He had over a dozen of them from many states and loved to show them off to his buddies. We kept the car in his garage. The Fiat I had sent him in 1975 had finally fallen apart, and he had sold it. He was a star. He had an "exotic" car from America in his care, and guys would congregate by the rows of garages to see it and discuss it. To Czechs, the Nissan Stanza was a very large car.

Because we brought a foreign-built car into the country, we had to pay "customs"—a penalty for not buying a Czech-made vehicle. Coming from America, it had to be changed to meet Czech standards of emissions and lights and be inspected every two years.

We bought insurance three months each time we visited, and my brother would take a train to the next town to pick up and return the license plates. No one else was brave enough to drive it when we were not there. They did not want to be responsible if something happened to it or to buy gas for it.

Getting parts for it was another story. Because that model was never imported to the Czech Republic or Europe, we had to bring parts from America. We packed them into our suitcases, and they always raised questions when we went through airport security. We took an air filter, an oil filter, (looked like a grenade) and even a headlight! Of course today nothing like that would be allowed.

In 1999, our worst fear was realized. We were going to visit Jon, my friend whom we had last visited in Germany and had since moved back to the Czech Republic. We were well past Prague on the highway, when the car engine just died. When I tried to restart it, I heard metallic sounds like *ping, ping*. We coasted to an exit ramp where a repair shop just happened to be at the end of it. Mechanics there also tried to get it started with the same results, actually causing more engine damage. We called Jon and he offered to come get us and tow the Stanza to his place with a rope. We tied it to his Opel Ascona, not a big car, and despite the rope breaking two times, we finally got to his home. Another miracle!

His mechanic did not know anything about Nissans, so we arranged to have it towed back to Nyrsko, about three hundred kilometers (186 miles). There, I did find a dealer who was willing to fix it if we supplied the parts. When we got back home to Florida, we bought $1000 in parts to rebuild the engine, and shipped them to my brother. Two months later, he picked up the car.

As the economy in the Czech Republic improved, more parts became available. A Nissan dealer opened and we were able to get future repairs done right there.

Because the Stanza was considered "exotic" we were always careful where we parked, and we secured the steering wheel with a locked club. Over the fifteen years that we owned the car there, we made many trips to Moravia and Germany, chauffeured people to doctor appointments and shopping, and picked up hitchhikers. We put over fifteen thousand kilometers (9320 miles) on the car.

Eventually, my brother couldn't care for it anymore. It was still in great shape, so in 2012 we donated it to the local church so they could pick up people outside of town for their church service. After that, we flew into Prague and rented cars—no inspections or maintenance to worry about.

Czech Update

Chapter 38

In the Czech Republic and many other European countries, people celebrate "name days." The calendars list one name for each day of the year, and it is celebrated like a birthday with congratulations, gifts, and alcohol. So everyone gets two special days a year. Everyone named Ladis celebrates June 27, and even Pat has a day for her name.

Many people who escaped have returned to live in Czechoslovakia again. Several of our friends have pensions from careers in Germany and enjoy a comfortable life. Jon bought a big house in Litomerice and travels frequently. My long-time friend Martin had escaped to Germany and also returned to Nyrsko. He is a very prosperous businessman and owns much property.

The previously forbidden border areas have been cleared and sold for new housing settlements. Some farmers receive government subsidies for grazing cattle and working the land. Eco-tourism and farms are promoted. People are encouraged to build guest accommodations, horse trails, and golf courses to attract tourists. The beautiful forests are now accessible to anyone to enjoy unspoiled nature.

Nyrsko has seen a lot of changes. From 1989 until 2013, it was a very prosperous town. Because it is so close to the border, Germans used to come into town to hair salons, eyeglass stores, restaurants, gas stations, and shops to get less expensive goods. There were over a dozen places to eat, and it was a very busy village. Recently both countries' economies have been struggling, and traffic has really decreased. All but four restaurants have closed and other businesses have shut down. Any restaurant must now meet European Union standards, which often requires the owner to renovate and update kitchens and bathrooms. Many cannot afford the expense and have closed.

After the fall of Communism, the Czech Republic was very attractive to Western interests, Germany, England, France, and Austria. Conditions were prime for foreign investors to build manufacturing plants. Inexpensive labor, low taxes, and government incentives were drawing new business into the Czech Republic.

In Nyrsko alone, there are four new foreign-owned plants employing hundreds of local people. The economy has benefited somewhat. A new outdoor skating rink and inline skating trail through the woods have been built.

Some people commute to low-wage jobs in Germany every day. Because of the Schengen Agreement, among the members of the European Union, it is possible for them to obtain jobs anywhere in Europe. They are paid in euros, which are more widely accepted than Czech currency, the koruna. Bars and casinos are doing well though; people are willing to spend their money on those.

The previously underground church is free to worship and has several branches. Right now they are meeting in a school. We have met missionaries from America and other countries who have visited and helped the church. Mormons, Jehovah Witnesses, and other religions have also come into the country.

Vietnamese immigrants own restaurants, and stores are full of inexpensive clothing and shoes; they outnumber Czech-owned businesses in some towns. Grocery stores have a good variety, almost anything you would find in a United States market.

Food and alcohol prices are much less than in the States, but gas is expensive. It is sold by the liter and works out to about $5 a gallon. Fast-food chains are appearing: Turkish kebab, Chinese food, pizza, Kentucky Fried Chicken, and McDonald's.

My brother-in-law is a farmer and sells his produce to stores now. There is low property tax on homes or businesses; thrift stores and coffee shops are thriving. There is a great deal of depravity and a lack of morals. Freedom is a good thing, but as in the United States, it creates other problems. What we consider pornography in America is sometimes shown on television at night in the Czech Republic.

The worst American movies and TV shows are shown; magazines and newspapers freely show nudity and have articles on sex and perversion. Children grow up too fast and have their own children, many without marriage. Adultery is frequent and destroys families and relationships. Money and material possessions are gods.

Business is sometimes done by lying, cheating, stealing, or bribery. A childhood friend of mine struggled in his heavy equipment business in Prague. Organized crime monopolized the business around the capital, so Ludvik had to travel far for a little work that did not pay well. He was hopeless and overwhelmed by debt. We helped him with his bills, but it was too little, too late. One day, in desperation, he killed himself. I was devastated. Ludvik always jokingly promised that he would ring my doorbell in America someday. Now it will never happen.

Under Communism there was a saying: "Who doesn't steal, steals from his own family." Sadly, today that still holds true for some people. The people now have the freedom to do almost anything but no moral compass to guide them.

Under Communism, we were forced to learn Russian. I tried not to, but after five years of it, a lot of it stuck in my brain. I started learning Italian and English in the camp, and I understand some languages from other Eastern Bloc countries.

I picked up some German from my dad and continued studying it in the States. Pat learned some French in school and studies German with me now. She knows enough Czech to make people laugh and to get by.

We live in Florida where many Europeans vacation, and we have had chances to chat with some of them. We learned of a mission opportunity in Austria where my knowledge of Russian—the language I hated to learn—can be used. No experience is wasted; God can use it for His good!

Chapter 39

Every year now around May 9 (Liberation Day) a parade of American military vehicles and personnel in US uniforms come into many towns in Bohemia. They are invited by the town officials to honor the American army who liberated that part of Czechoslovakia.

Plaques commemorating General Patton's Third Army division were mounted on city halls after the war but were removed and hidden from the Communists until 1989. Now they are decorated with Czech and American flags for the event. Speeches are given in the larger towns where they stop; sometimes an official from the American embassy is there. The jeeps and other Army vehicles have been carefully restored by Czechs who retrieved them and worked on them secretly for years.

"Soldiers" are enthusiasts from other countries in US uniforms. One year, we were in Nyrsko when the group came through and we talked with them. One trooper was actually from Pennsylvania, but the others were from Scotland and Germany. Families came out to see the vehicles, and the children heard the truth about who liberated that part of Czechoslovakia.

Under Communism we were taught that the Russian Red Army liberated the whole country, which was a lie! Patton and his troops were responsible for freeing western Bohemia from the Nazis. In Nyrsko, and in the whole region, everybody knew this fact but could not acknowledge it or discuss it publicly. To do so would have been very dangerous and punishable by fine or jail or both.

Our mission to the Czech Republic continues today.

This year, we are planning parties at both ends of the Czech Republic for our 40th wedding anniversary. These celebrations will be for my family because they couldn't come to the wedding in Massachusetts.

The first party will be in a small castle with a dozen relatives. Pat will be wearing a light blue German dirndl dress with lace from her first wedding gown. She made her original headpiece into a halo of flowers and ribbons. I am wearing a jacket similar to my original tuxedo.

The second party will have thirty guests—family and dear friends—whom we have known for decades. We will have a beautiful lighted arch behind us, candles, soft music, elegant food, beautiful cakes, and champagne. Vases of lilacs will line the tables.

Besides renewing our vows, in Czech, we hope to show that a marriage based on love and respect can endure and still be fun even after four decades. We will give God the glory for our time together and His protection and provision in our lives.

We continue encouraging and helping people however we can. My hatred of the Communists and the oppression of Czechoslovakia was the catalyst for my leaving, but God had a purpose in it: to do a greater good by escaping and returning. We praise Him for His guidance and love and mercy. As Joseph in Genesis 50:20 says, "You intended to harm me, but God intended it for good, to accomplish what is now being done . . ."

Liberation Day celebrations, Nyrsko

Liberation Day celebrations, Nyrsko

"For I know the plans I have for you," declares the Lord, "plans to prosper you and not to harm you, plans to give you hope and a future" (Jeremiah 29:11).

I grew up in a small town outside of Boston, Massachusetts, and had never heard of Czechoslovakia. I loved fairy tales and castles and dreamed of studying fashion in Paris someday. The only "foreigners" I knew were exchange students who came to my school. Although I liked the sounds of accents, I didn't know one from another.

In the 1970s I was living in Boston and decided to move to New York City. I knew two people there. One was a brother of a friend, and I stayed with him and his roommate until I got a job and moved in with three girls.

Eventually I got my own place—a fifth-floor walk-up apartment—and I met Ladis at a volleyball game. He was the most interesting person I had ever met, and the most handsome too!

He had a strong accent and would not tell me what he did for work. So when he picked me up for our first date in a big Cadillac and drove me to the woods of Bear Mountain, I was a little scared and figured he was Mafia! I thought I was going to be assaulted, and I could hear my mother's words echoing in my head about being careful with strangers in the big city. But he was a perfect gentleman. He built a campfire, grilled sausages, and we swam in the lake. He was not like anyone I had ever met before, and two years later we were married. That was just the beginning of our adventures.

New York was as far as I had been outside of New England, so our first trip to Czechoslovakia in 1977 was a real shock to me. I thought everyone had hot running water, flush toilets, and all the food that was available in our grocery stores. I now know how blessed my childhood in America was.

Ladis and I came from such different cultures and family situations. One of his Czech friends encouraged him not to marry an American, saying it "would never work." Yet she came to America with her Czech husband and then divorced him. God has woven us together for His purposes. It has been amazing to experience Europe and the changes over the years, to see such beautiful countries with centuries-old histories. We share a love for languages and exploring, having visited dozens of castles with so many more to see.

My family also needed our help. My dad died when we were living in Jupiter, Florida, and we decided to move back to Massachusetts, which ended up being for another twenty years. My brother died from alcoholism, and my mother had dementia and was going blind.

When she was in her eighties she allowed us to take over her care. She relied on Ladis to fix the television remote that she could not see clearly anymore, put tennis balls on her walker, and fix the vacuum after she had sucked up a necklace.

We had many stressful years as we juggled her issues, our own lives, and the family overseas. I do not think she understood us, but she did admire Ladis. She admitted to us one day that for a long time, she had thought he was a spy, but then decided he was not one after all. We did the best we could for her until she passed away at ninety-five.

We decided to move back to Florida where we have a busy retirement. We hope to keep traveling for quite a while and see what the Lord has in store for us. We are excited about this book and hope to have it translated into Czech and German so the younger generations will know what Communism was like and, hopefully, never take their freedom for granted.

Thank you for reading it and God bless you!

—Pat Visner

"Communism works only in heaven, where they don't need it, and in hell, where they already have it."

—Ronald Reagan

www.ingramcontent.com/pod-product-compliance
Lightning Source LLC
Chambersburg PA
CBHW061733050726
47598CB00002B/465